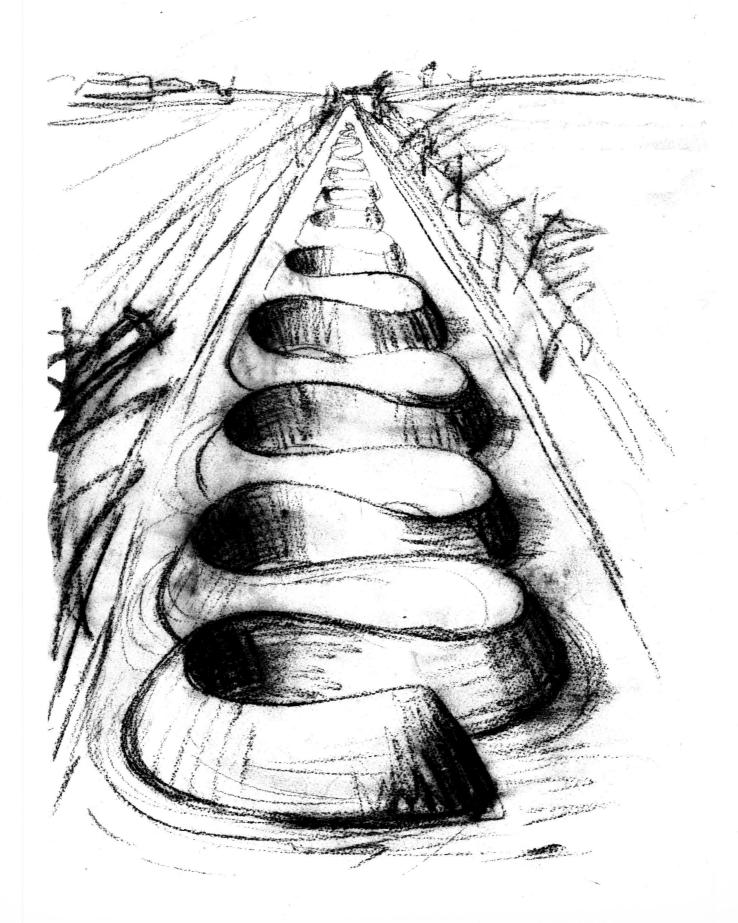

40 Under 40
THE NEW GENERATION IN BRITAIN

Andy Goldsworthy, *Slate Hole*, 1987

Original Graphic

ANDY GOLDSWORTHY

An original graphic created by Andy Goldsworthy as a
preliminary study for his recent *Lambton Earthwork*.

Antony Gormley, *As Above So Below*, 1987-8, lead, fibreglass, plaster, air

An Art & Design Profile

40 Under 40
THE NEW GENERATION IN BRITAIN

Helen Chadwick, *The Oval Court*, 1986, installation

ACADEMY EDITIONS·LONDON/ST. MARTIN'S PRESS·NEW YORK

Acknowledgements

Front Cover: Peter Randall-Page, *Cone and Vessel*, 1988, Forest of Dean Stone, courtesy Forest of Dean Sculpture Project. *Back Cover*: Richard Wilson, *Leading Lights*, 1988, courtesy Matt's Gallery; *Inside Front Cover*: Suzanne Treister, *Time Machine*, 1988, oil, courtesy Edward Totah Gallery; *Inside Back Cover*: Lance Smith, *Icarus*, 1988, mixed media, courtesy Fabian Carlsson Gallery; *Half-Title*: Andy Goldsworthy, *Slate Hole*, 1987, courtesy Fabian Carlsson Gallery/ Galleria Cavini Florence ; *Frontis*: Antony Gormley, *As Above So Below*, 1987-8, lead, fibreglass, plaster, air, courtesy the artist; *Title*: Helen Chadwick, *The Oval Court*, 1986, installation, courtesy the artist; *Contents*: Veronica Ryan, *Surfacing*, 1988, bronze, courtesy Kettle's Yard Cambridge

We should like to thank all the individual artists and galleries who supplied material for this issue. We should also like to thank the following for their help and advice: Bryan Kneale at the RCA, Andrew Nairne at the Third Eye Centre Glasgow, Peter Jones at the Welsh Arts Council, Declan McGonnegal Director, Orchard Gallery Derry, Rob La Frenais for his advice on performance art, Caroline Collier at the South Bank Centre, Richard Humphries and Frances Morris at the Tate Gallery

Current Trends
pp6-7: Illustration courtesy Raab Gallery.
The New British Painting
pp8-15: This article takes its title from the exhibition, *The New British Painting*, jointly curated by Carolyn Cohen and Edward Lucie-Smith, originating at the Contemporary Arts Center, Cincinnati in November 1988 and subsequently touring to Chicago Public Library Cultural Center; Haggerty Museum, Marquette University, Milwaukee; Southeastern Center for Contemporary Art, Winston-Salem; Grand Rapids Art Museum, Michigan; Queens Museum, New York. We are grateful to the publishers of *The New British Painting* co-published by Phaidon, Oxford, and the Contemporary Arts Center, Cincinnati, 1988 (paperback £9.95) for permission to reproduce Carolyn Cohen's essay and several of the illustrations which appear in this volume.
Art to Tease the Mind
pp38-42: Ian Hughes, Philip Braham and Richard Gilbert courtesy Raab Gallery, Lucy Ross

courtesy Sue Williams.
New Irish Art from Recent Exhibitions
pp50-51: Illustrations supplied by Willie Doherty, Micky Donnelly, Chris Wilson.
Freeze
pp52-3: Illustrations provided by Angela Bulloch.
Spaces, Places and Landmarks: Environmental Art
pp54-8: Illustrations of works in the Forest of Dean provided by Rupert Martin, organiser of the Forest of Dean Sculpture Project in collaboration with Martin Orrom of the Forestry Commission, illustrations of works by Simon Thomas courtesy the artist and Albemarle Gallery.
Generation Games in Sculpture
pp62-5: Illustrations are from the following: Kapoor from the exhibition *British Sculpture 1960-1988*, Museum van Hedendgaagse Kunst Antwerpen, January - March 1989, Cragg from the exhibition, *Tony Cragg*, Tate Gallery London, April - June 1989, Houshiari courtesy Lisson Gallery.
New Art in Wales
pp70-73: Illustrations supplied by David Briers and the artists, works by Emrys Williams courtesy Benjamin Rhodes.
Disparate Pockets
pp76-9: Simon Herbert is a performance and video artist and regular contributor to *Performance* and *High Performance*, he is currently co-organiser of Projects UK in Newcastle-upon-Tyne which commissions time-based art.
New Contemporaries, New Talent
pp80-81: Illustrations courtesy Christie's South Kensington and James Hockey Gallery, West Surrey College of Art and Design Farnham.
Checklist
pp82-3: Illustrations provided by the artists except those provided by the following galleries: Berkeley Square for Achache, Paton for Calland, Long & Ryle for Conway Jones, Lisson for Davey, Raab for Hosie, Karston Schubert for Landy, Fabian Carlsson for O'Donoghue, Third Eye Centre for Sullivan, Riverside Studios for Wilson; Hatoum and Rolfe from *Edge 88*.

———— * ————

CHRISTOPHER LE BRUN p8 courtesy Nigel Greenwoood/Contemporary Arts Center Cincinnati; **THERESE OULTON** p16 courtesy Marlborough Fine Art; **KAREN FORSYTH** p17 courtesy Albemarle Gallery; **LOUISE BLAIR** p17 courtesy the artist and Nicola Jacobs Gallery; **STEPHEN FARTHING** p18-19 courtesy the artist; **JOHN KEANE** p20 courtesy Angela Flowers; **KEN CURRIE** p20 courtesy Raab Gallery; **PAUL STOREY** p21 courtesy Fischer Fine Art; **KEITH MCINTYRE** p21 courtesy Raab Gallery; **SARAH RAPHAEL** p22-3 courtesy Agnew's; **SONIA BOYCE** p24 this text is an extract from an article by the artist in the catalogue to accompany the exhibition *The Impossible Self* curated by Bruce Ferguson and Sandy Nairne at Winnipeg Art Gallery, Canada, April-July 1988, and reproduced courtesy Sonia Boyce, Sandy Nairne and Winnipeg Art Gallery, the illustration is from the exhibition *Sonia Boyce: Recent Work*, Whitechapel Art Gallery, May-June 1988; **GRAHAM DEAN** p25 courtesy Austin/Desmond Fine Art; **MADELEINE STRINDBERG** pp26-7 photos Edward Woodman, we are also grateful to the National Gallery for their help; **LANCE SMITH** p28 courtesy Fabian Carlsson; **JONATHAN WALLER** p29 courtesy Paton Gallery; **ANDREW CARNIE** p30-31 courtesy the artist; **MARK WALLINGER** p32 courtesy Anthony Reynolds Gallery; **ADRIAN WISZNIEWSKI** p33-4 this painting was specially commissioned for the symposium British Art Now, Academy Forum at the Tate 1988, photo Dave Lambert; **RICHARD DEACON** p35-6 illustrations courtesy the retrospective exhibition, *Richard Deacon*, Whitechapel Art Gallery November 1988-January

1989; **DAVID MACH** p37 courtesy the artist, photo of *Tamed Trained Framed* Arthur Foster; **JANE LANGLEY** p38 courtesy the artist; **ANSEL KRUT** p42 courtesy Fischer Fine Art; **LUCY ROSS** p43 courtesy Sue Williams; **HELEN CHADWICK** pp44-6 courtesy the artist, photo p44 Edward Woodman; **ANDY GOLDSWORTHY** pp47-8 courtesy Fabian Carlsson; **WILLIE DOHERTY** p49 courtesy the artist; **PETER RANDALL-PAGE** p54 courtesy Common Ground, New Milestones Project; **CHRIS DRURY** and **KATE WHITEFORD** pp59-61 courtesy the artists; **SHIRAZEH HOUSHIARY** p62 courtesy Lisson Gallery, photo Tomasz Samek/SQB; **ANTONY GORMLEY** p66 the text is based on an interview with the artist by Miranda Argyle. These works were part of an exhibition in 1989 of Antony Gormley's work at the Louisiana Museum Denmark touring to the Scottish National Gallery of Modern Art; **EDWARD ALLINGTON** p67 courtesy the artist and the Lisson Gallery, photos Edward Woodman; **NICOLA HICKS** p68 courtesy Angela Flowers; **VERONICA RYAN** p69 courtesy the artist from the recent exhibition at Kettle's Yard Cambridge; **CALUM COLVIN** p74 courtesy Salama Caro; **MICHAEL PETRY** p74 illustrations of the 1988 installations *Chaos Human Atomica* at Unit 7 and *Parallel Works* at Adam Gallery supplied by the artist; **RICHARD WILSON** p75 *Leading Lights*, courtesy the artist and Matt's Gallery, *20:50* courtesy Saatchi Collection; **ANDRE STITT** p76 courtesy the artist, photo Covert Activities; **STEPHEN TAYLOR WOODROW** p79 photo supplied by Tracey Warr.

Editor: Dr Andreas C Papadakis

First published in Great Britain in 1989 by *Art & Design*
an imprint of the
ACADEMY GROUP LTD, 7 HOLLAND STREET, LONDON W8 4NA
ISBN: 0-85670-995-6 (UK)
Art & Design Profile 14 is published as part of *Art & Design* Vol 5 3/4-1989
Published in the United States of America by
ST MARTIN'S PRESS, 175 FIFTH AVENUE, NEW YORK 10010
ISBN: 0-312-03160-2(USA)
Printed and bound in Singapore

Contents

Veronica Ryan, *Surfacing*, 1988, bronze

With contributions by
John McEwan on Stephen Farthing, Alistair Hicks on Sarah Raphael,
Colin Wiggins on Madeleine Strindberg, Sue Williams on her Gallery, Mark Holborn on Helen Chadwick,
Angela Bulloch on *Freeze*, David Reason on Chris Drury and Kate Whiteford

CHRISTOPHER LE BRUN

Christopher Le Brun, *Tree with Hill*, 1987, oil

THE NEW BRITISH PAINTING
Carolyn Cohen

Ken Currie, *Workshop of the World* (*Hope and Optimism in Spite of Present Difficulties*), 1987, oil

Interest in young British artists has spread across the Atlantic as seen by *The New British Painting* exhibition, organised by Cincinnati Contemporary Arts Center, currently touring the United States. Carolyn Cohen its joint curator discusses reasons contributing to this enthusiasm, in particular the emphasis on figuration and narrative and the legacy of the 19th-century landscape tradition, and presents the work of over 20 younger artists.

The decade of the 1980s has witnessed a burgeoning new vitality in British art. In a climate where the visual arts have never been held in the same esteem as literature, drama or music, the attention currently focused on painting and sculpture suggests that the visual arts are beginning to find an appreciative audience and, at a gradual but steady pace, gain their rightful status.

A number of factors in Britain account for this critical shift. Certainly, the opportunities for viewing art are increasing: commercial galleries and alternative spaces are proliferating, particularly in London, and many exhibitions have been organised and circulated throughout Britain. The emergence of Scotland as a centre of prodigious activity has broadened the scope of British art, and energised the London art market. Further evidence of interest and support is shown by the public who, after taking their lead from a few important collectors, seem willing to buy contemporary art. And a dedicated group of art critics continues to enliven the print and broadcast media and help to mitigate the customary tide of resistance to the visual arts.

This revitalisation is very much a product of a new *Zeitgeist* of the 1980s. Having been for so long its own worst enemy, the British artworld is beginning to shed the vestiges of its inferiority complex. Undoubtedly, contemporary British artists have been a galvanising force in the recovery of British confidence and national identity. For one thing, New York no longer serves British artists as their primary reference point, as it has in previous decades. Nor do these artists feel compelled to defend or qualify their position against an international background.

The artists in this exhibition share a common concern for humanism. Much of the work is, therefore, figurative. While it could be argued that the landscape painters tend toward abstraction, their imagery, nonetheless, remains rooted in natural forms. The most immediate source for British figurative painting in the 1980s is the 'School of London' (Francis Bacon, Lucian Freud, Leon Kossoff, Frank Auerbach, R B Kitaj and Michael Andrews), a group of artists who formed a nucleus of the Tate Gallery's 1984 exhibition *The Hard-Won Image*.[1] Eschewing the abstraction of the 1950s, these artists struggled to sustain the continuity of the British figurative tradition in the midst of a hostile environment. In claiming the pre-eminence of these modern masters, *The Hard-Won Image* put forth a strong case for the return of figuration as one of.the most important elements of contemporary British painting.

The common cultural identity of the new generation has nurtured an aesthetic which is 'issue-oriented', as well as figurative. These issues, while based on a personal vision, are often derived from broader cultural, social or historical arenas. A curious feature of these artists is their tendency to search for appropriate models from the past to interpret ideas of the present. For example, ties to 19th-century British painting are apparent in their approach to the subject of landscape. But sources other than the British past are equally prevalent. It is less a characteristic of eclecticism and more a function of their academic training and access to important public collections, that accounts for their wealth of art-historical references. Certain artists adopt the formal vocabularies of early 20th-century movements, such as French Fauvism or German *Neue Sachlichkeit* (New Objectivity), into their imagery, while the Classical tradition, as it survived into the late 19th century, is both revered and rigidly practised among younger artists.

Especially relevant in the context of this exhibition is the American response to contemporary British painting. The current wave of interest among the British in their new generation of painters was stimulated, in part, by enterprising American curators, dealers and collectors who, in the beginning of the 1980s, played *deus ex machina*. This intervention resulted in not only the representation of even the most risky work in important US collections and exhibitions; it also forced the British art world to take notice of its own bright stars. It is significant, for example, that Steven Campbell, who initiated the present activity and attention focused on Glasgow, established his reputation first in New York.

That the American interest has boosted the credibility of the new British painting in Britain is, perhaps, best perceived as an indication of the greater receptivity within the US (for better or worse) to new developments in contemporary art. The American appetite for new British painting, however, suggests that these works satisfy a certain longing for a content-based imagery.

indicative of the predominant currents in contemporary British painting, became evident. The artists were chosen from among scores of immensely gifted and inventive painters because they synthesise, in our view, those characteristics which individuate their national identity. One such characteristic is the reinstatement of the importance of subject-matter, manifested in an overwhelming concern for humanism, expressed through a variety of ways. No less apparent, however, is the vigour with which they freely set forth their own ideas about the nature of painting.

Certain shared ideologies and subjects provide a framework for grouping these artists thematically. They are discussed, therefore, individually within four broad overlapping categories. These are: Still Life, Landscape, elaboration of Personal Mythology and Social Concerns.

Still Life
Both John Monks and Lisa Milroy are painters of objects extracted from the commonplace or familiar. These objects are dissociated from their original contexts, stripped of utility and function, and relocated into settings which alter their symbolic values. These artists share a somewhat abstractionist approach to

 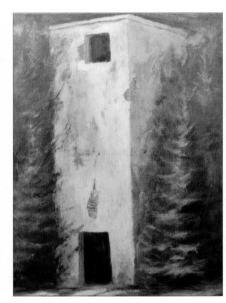 

L to R: Campbell, *'Twas Once an Architect's Office in Wee Nook*, 1984; Barclay, *Night Tower*, 1987; Conroy, *Wireless Vision Accomplished*, 1987

Ironically, Britain's insularity and previous lack of a supportive environment for its artists may account for the high degree of originality and integrity characteristic to its painting. This imagery seems to thrive on an innovation that is more evolutionary than exploratory. The work can be ingenuous and forthright without being simplistic. While it is often arcane, it is not remote and even at its most introspective it offers a connective thread to the outside world.

The New British Painting is an overview of British painting of the 1980s. By no means exhaustive or comprehensive, it is a preamble to a larger movement in progress. The 26 artists included in the exhibition all live and work primarily in Britain where they received their artistic training. They range in age from 24 to 42. Many of them, therefore, began their careers in the present decade. As a collective body they form a postscript to the 1987 exhibition, *British Art in the 20th Century*, organised by the Royal Academy of Arts, London. They are likely, however, to be remembered in surveys of art of the 21st century.

The artists selected for inclusion in the exhibition form no coherent group, nor do they represent any single direction. In the process of selection, however, certain similarities in their work,

content, although their concerns are not entirely formal. They are highly innovative within a still-life tradition which, in the case of Monks and Milroy, seems too limited a category.

Monks' excavation sites are London's rubbish heaps, where he finds discarded bits of clothing, appliances or car parts. All of these things, created by and for human beings, had a former life. They are fashioned by the artist into *memento mori*, reminders of death. Objects are re-assigned to his studio, where Monks sets out to 'construct (for them) an environment, an atmosphere, some kind of mood or interior'.[2] The artist's presence is detected in the studied, Classical order of his compositions and the infusion of artificial, theatrical lighting that adumbrates some forms and illuminates the rich textures of others. Although he describes his objects with painstaking precision, Monks skilfully manages to avoid preciosity.

By contrast, Milroy, who paints objects from memory, intentionally withholds clues about their original contexts or relocation. Her paintings convey a strong sense of detachment, as they are about things twice removed from experience. Milroy avoids consistency in perspective, and the neutral space which contains her objects could be an imaginary wall or a floor. A subtle, homogeneous source of light provides the whispered tonalities that illusionistically describe the volume of her objects. Milroy looks at things as representations of a class or species, defined by appearance rather than essence. In *Fragments,* she depicts individual pieces of Greek pottery, set apart from one another. The artist's fascination with regimentation is denoted in *Shirts,* where she repeats a single motif as a series, lined up in contiguous uniform rows.

Landscape

Landscape painting forms a particularly cherished part of the history of British art. The impact of J M W Turner and John Constable was felt in later developments, most notably Impressionism, and their legacy extends to artists of the present day whose subject is landscape. The temptation to draw comparisons and search for models in the 19th century is great, and some contemporary painters freely acknowledge these sources of inspiration. Certainly, paintings of landscape in the exhibition are highly romantic in tone. And implicit in these romantic images are traces of the 18th- and 19th-century notion of the 'sublime' in nature, where a natural world is portrayed as

proportions of the human figure (his and the viewer's), and by technique, through which he conveys a sense of immediate physical activity and presence. McKeever's compositions begin with a collage of torn sections of black-and-white photographs, which are enlarged to show close-up details of the specific landscape. The painting-over process which follows is McKeever's attempt to 'relocate that image as painting'.[4] Thus, like Turner, he combines direct observation with memory. In his experimental handling of materials, which signals a concern for achieving an authenticity of expression, the artist is closer to Constable, whose landscapes, McKeever claims, become 'abstract' more quickly.

In contrast to McKeever who seeks out exotic locations for his landscapes, John Virtue's sole subject is the tiny hamlet of Green Haworth in the Lancashire moorlands, where he has lived and worked for the past two decades. Virtue's interest is not in recording especially transient conditions of climate or other powerful natural phenomena. He is content, instead, to explore the multiple perspectives which offer infinite possibilities for experiencing an isolated bit of landscape. His individual, miniature variations on a single theme (a thicket, house or farm) are

L to R: Amanda Faulkner, *Inside Out*, 1985, acrylic; Gwen Hardie, *The Brave One*, 1987, oil

picturesque and beautiful on the one hand, and terrifying and powerful, on the other. More striking than the shared thematic interest, however, are the similarities in material sensibilities between contemporary landscape painters and their precursors. Both Constable's emphasis on nature's abstract elements, and Turner's concern for the struggle between the elements which resulted in the dissolution of a material reality where the recognisable subject ultimately disappears, are evident, in varying degrees, in the work of Ian McKeever, Thérèse Oulton and Christopher Le Brun. The influence of another painter of landscape, Samuel Palmer, is apparent in the obsessive, intimately scaled, pastoral studies of John Virtue.

Ian McKeever travels to remote, primeval locations in search of landscapes that inspire both wonder and terror. The Island of Staffa in the Inner Hebrides, unique for its majestic, volcanically formed caves, was the site for perilous expeditions in the 19th century by English painters and poets, such as Turner and Keats. Unlike Turner, who approached Fingal's Cave as a vista and 'blurred it into a broader landscape', McKeever transports us directly into the midst of the towering rock formations.[3] He achieves this effect both by scale, as he adjusts the space to the

assembled in a grid-like serial fashion. They are meant to be read as a unified composite image, rather than as a sequential narrative. Although he uses traditional drawing media, Virtue considers his intricate, labour-intensive compositions as 'painterly'. This effect is generated by his dense web of cross-hatched lines through which he also achieves a Rembrandt-like chiaroscuro. Though Rembrandt's etchings are an inspiration to Virtue, another source for his imagery, closer to home, is Samuel Palmer. Palmer not only produced tiny, compact pastoral studies in etching; he also pursued an obsessive scrutiny of a particular place.

Thérèse Oulton's concern is with the 'properties of the natural world, but from within'.[5] Oulton turns the natural world inside out by unearthing its inner workings of subterranean dark and secret places. A tension between the physical and spiritual exists in her work which hovers on the boundary between figuration and abstraction. Oulton appears to be proceeding methodically toward the removal of recognisable imagery in her recent paintings, claiming that recognition inhibits the imagination. What appeals to Oulton in the landscapes of Turner and Constable is their abstractionist presentation and transformation of material processes. Oulton performs an alchemist's magic in transforming nature into art. Her gem-like, encrusted surfaces are achieved through an inventive combination of *alla prima* and glazing. In this way Oulton portrays nature, always mysterious, as both ephemeral and eternal.

The images that materialise in Christopher Le Brun's work are the result of an autogenetic process that takes place during the act of painting. For Le Brun, strokes of paint are both abstract and associative. A single mark might suggest the head of a horse or branch of a tree. While these motifs have a significance that is not entirely formal, the artist, whose faith is in the innateness of his imagery to the picture, has stated: 'Painting is a kind of mask for my subjects which I will not discuss.'[6] Like others of his contemporaries who explore the subject of landscape, Le Brun vacillates between abstraction and figuration, though elements of both consistently recur in his work. The point of departure for his unpremeditated paintings is, however, his imagination. Le Brun describes himself as 'by temperament . . . a visionary painter after Turner and Blake'.[7] And, in the manner of these artists, he creates a tension between the actual and the visionary, from which his monumental paintings derive their power.

Amanda Faulkner explores the multi-faceted female personality by representing women in a panoply of traditionally ascribed roles. Her characters are often versions of the same woman, as in *Inside Out*. The primitive icon, 'feminised' by a ridiculous hair ribbon, edges into the foreground, where a comatose woman appears as little more than a stylish-looking automaton. Surrounded by those with whom she is interdependent, and consequently, about whom she is ambivalent, Faulkner's woman is both consumed and defined by her relationships with others. Male demons masquerading as babies express the artist's abnegation of the mythic role of woman as benevolent nurturer. Faulkner is clearly out to subvert the traditional Madonna and Child fantasy of the male artist. The detached organs that float absurdly in space remind us that women are tyrannised by their own bodies.

Like Faulkner, Gwen Hardie has in mind the formulation of a depictive language that offers an alternative to the female prototypes developed by male artists. Her monumental, blown-up anatomical details communicate her ambition to re-invent the female body, inch by inch, from the woman's point of view. In her painting, *The Brave One,* Hardie concentrates on the external

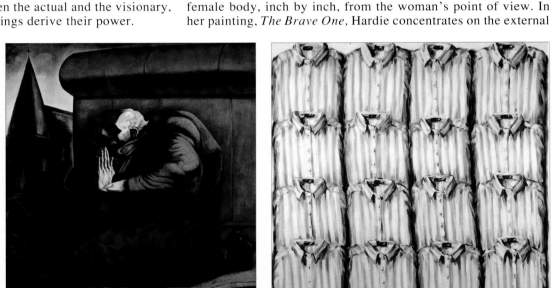

L to R: John Monks, *Car Door*, 1986, oil; Peter Howson, *A Wing and a Prayer*, 1987, oil; Lisa Milroy, *Shirts*, 1986, oil

Personal Mythology

Those paintings in the exhibition considered to be the elaboration of a personal mythology are not so much direct representations of an artist's own experience, as they are the artist's emotional and highly personal response to a situation. The figures in these revealing works are quite often both self-portrait and *alter ego*. Sometimes, the imagery recreates a state of mind, or describes a sentiment in the form of allegory. While the impetus for these paintings is always personal, they contain images which can be decoded universally. Amanda Faulkner and Gwen Hardie share a concern for recording the psychological and physical conditions of womanhood, while Eileen Cooper and Mary Mabbutt are inspired by scenes from their everyday lives. Stephen Conroy refers to the 19th-century academic tradition which informs his personal ideas about the nature of painting, while Stephen Barclay looks to contemporary German artists who similarly treat the subject of the aftermath of war. Andrzej Jackowski, Simon Edmondson and Adrian Wiszniewski depict interior visions which deal with memories of sensory experience, rather than individual incidents from their pasts, in paintings intended both to capture and evoke a mood of reverie.

aspects of her body, re-creating the skin's surface as pigment. The artist forges a tactile, immediate relationship with her images by using the body's own tools – her fingers – to apply and mould the paint directly on to the canvas. Although she uses her own body as a reference point, Hardie's 'self-identifications' are not in the least narcissistic. Rather, they are resolute statements of female authority, underscored by her active presence as both subject and artist.

The rationale for Eileen Cooper's paintings, which revolve around women as central figures, is 'to make sense of my life, to celebrate it'.[8] Cooper's work maintains a strong sense of narrative when read as a succession of images acting as entries in a visual diary. The artist combines mask-like faces reminiscent of Picasso with a vivid Fauvist palette to reproduce a primitive state of the imagination that is not, she states, 'restricted to a logical description of the world'.[9] While autobiographical in inspiration, Cooper's stories are meant to be more universal in implication. Closely paralleling events in her own life, Cooper's imagery has evolved from monumental, generic mother-and-child paintings to intimately scaled, direct depictions of a single female figure. Often, as in *If the Shoe Fits,* the figure is engaged in some mundane female ritual. As a concept both new and unknown to the artist, motherhood assumed mythic proportions; as an activity, it became increasingly demystified. In *Babies,* the infants who occupy a space in the background of the painting, are now viewed as just one part of a woman's life, rather than as the phenomena which traditionally bind women to a limited cultural definition.

Mary Mabbutt's paintings are also re-creations of moments from her own experience. Unlike Cooper's images, however, Mabbutt's transcriptions of events are more literal than allegorical. While memorable to the artist, these events are often quite ordinary and the impulse to paint them arises spontaneously. Mabbutt exploits the manner in which clothing can convey a mood or sensation. In *Walking on the Beach,* her bulky overcoat conjures up the cold, harsh climate of Falmouth, the artist's home in southwest England. Mabbutt also employs clothing as a pictorial device, and reduces familiar items of apparel, such as shoes, to arrangements of planar, fragmented forms. This concern for geometry aligns her with certain English artists of the early part of this century, such as Wyndham Lewis and Christopher Nevinson. The significance which she attaches to subject-

Stephen Barclay has converted the legacy of war and its aftermath into a personal mythology. The experience of World War II is inextricably woven into Barclay's family history, and his imagery is inspired by the indelible memories passed down by his parents, both of whom served in the Armed Forces. In *The Parachutist* and *Night Tower,* the artist isolates the solitary figure or architectural remnant in abandoned military sites, which cast what he calls 'war's permanent shadow' over the Scottish countryside.[12] Barclay integrates his preoccupation with war with his primary impulse as a painter of desolate, melancholy landscapes. In this way, he reveals his affinity with the modern generation of war-obsessed German artists, particularly Anselm Kiefer, whose influence Barclay acknowledges.

The paintings of Andrzej Jackowski elicit a mood of reverie that matches his interior visions of the ambiguous state between imagination and reality. For Jackowski, the facture of the painting is as provocative as the image portrayed. The artist brushes in suggestions of images with sepia, and gradually builds up the surfaces of his paintings with glazes through which he achieves the dreamlike effect of an ethereal luminosity. Many of the motifs found in Jackowski's imagery are intended as

L to R: Eileen Cooper, *If the Shoe Fits*, 1987, oil; Graham Crowley, *Peripheral Vision*, 1987, oil

matter, however, prevents her from moving further toward abstraction.

Stephen Conroy's paintings seem, at first glance, like anachronisms. The sombre, brooding atmosphere of his oppressive, stuffy interior scenes would place them more comfortably into a late-Victorian or early-Edwardian setting. They are uncompromisingly formal, down to the last detail of their ponderous 'period' frames. Furthermore, Conroy keeps them behind glass to deliberately 'cut them off' from the viewer.[10] What makes this prodigious artist (at 24, the youngest in the exhibition) at once curious and remarkable is his acute sense of composition, both rigidly ordered and restrained. In *167 Renfrew Street,* Conroy lets us into his private vision of a drawing class at the Glasgow School of Art, where young men are stiffly dressed in proper attire to denote the solemnity of the occasion. Firmly committed to the Classical tradition, and heir to the legacy of fine draughtsmanship associated with Scottish painting, Conroy uses this context to make a potent statement about academicism. Conroy admires Degas and Sickert for their 'sense of dissonance', or the way in which they could distill a mood of deep unrest out of their depictions of scenes from everyday life.[11]

metaphors for the retrieval of one's past.

Simon Edmondson's sumptuous, romantic paintings share with Jackowski's the ability to transport the viewer into another realm. The setting for Edmondson's images is the mental landscape in which the spiritual and the physical co-exist. The artist often uses colour (or the absence of it) and line not so much to distinguish one world from another, but rather to convey different shades and intensities of emotion. In *A Hundred Ardent Lovers Fell into Eternal Sleep* these distinctions become nebulous. Aroused by the act of love, the apparitions that crowd the earthbound lovers belong to a collective subconscious in which past and present lives are united.

Adrian Wiszniewski's paintings, like those of Jackowski and Edmondson, are best understood as depictions of dreamscapes, fraught with symbols that relate to a personal iconography. The subject of Wiszniewski's sensual and allegorical narratives is the restless state of adolescence. And the languorous youths who appear in his enigmatic scenes are the artist's *alter ego.* In a manner more graphic than painterly, Wiszniewski uses swirling ribbons of bright pigment to construct elaborate mazes that communicate the attendant confusions and ambivalent desires of pubescence. Filled with blossoming flowers and phallic imagery, the eroticised landscapes that surround Wiszniewski's figures are metaphors for diffused sexual passions. But his dizzying labyrinths are really intended to caution us that Wiszniewski's narratives, like irrational dreams, are not meant to be read logically. Even his titles are puzzles. *Nuclear Fission* might refer to the process of reproduction that occurs when atoms are split. It is, however, more likely about 'fishin'' and how a youthful mind transposes preposterous-sounding, meaningless concepts into an empirical framework.

Social Concerns

Contemporary painting based on social concerns runs the gamut from gentle satire to political propaganda. Both society and culture are the targets of this group of painters. Certain artists focus on a particular social class: John Keane, on the idiosyncrasies of London's new middle class; Jock McFadyen on its lower classes; Ken Currie and Peter Howson on realistic portrayals of Glasgow's impoverished working class. Kevin Sinnott explores social problems endemic to human nature, while Suzanne Treister, Tim Head and Graham Crowley use elaborate symbols to portray the grim, destructive elements that threaten contemporary society. The Post-Industrial age and its effects on the British value system are important to Steven Campbell and Jonathan Waller, while Mark Wallinger confronts the English national past head on.

John Keane's brand of social satire addresses 'the quirks and ironies of living in the 20th century'.[13] The target of his often humorous, sometimes caustic exposés is the modern breed of white-collar, socially mobile, salaried professional – the 'yuppie'. This prosperous new middle class rarely appears as a subject in British painting and it is an irony, which even the artist acknowledges, that Keane mocks the very segment of society that buys his work. In *Who You Are and What You Do,* he depicts a crush of well-appointed, faceless individuals in a chic London cocktail bar, as a modern parable of sex, drugs and money. Keane softens his diatribe and livens up his compositions with touches of wit and humour, achieved through technical devices such as energetic brushstrokes, oblique perpectives and collages of real objects applied on to the canvas.

A 50-pence ride on the London Underground is not all that separates Keane's smart West Enders from Jock McFadyen's gritty East Enders. Nowhere is this distance more acutely described than in McFadyen's images of working-class street life. His repertoire ranges from prostitutes, as in *Rainy Day Women, L8,* to hucksters, skinheads and mothers pushing prams. The common denominator is poverty. The artist attempts to simulate the objectivity of photography, from which he derives certain visual techniques, notably in the angles and spatial organisations of his compositions. The caricature and grotesquerie of his figures, as well as the brightness of his palette, provide moments of comic relief in otherwise grim portraits of spiritual neglect. McFadyen's dockside genre subjects are, for the most part, neither judgemental nor critical in tone. He assumes quite a different posture, however, in paintings drawn from his experience in Northern Ireland, which are unequivocally condemning of religious intolerance. In *Parade,* McFadyen uses caricature to mock the Orangemen (members of the Protestant sect) as they march through Belfast, portraying their leader as a pompous circus dog, decked out in Lodgeman's finery.

Ken Currie and Peter Howson focus on the problems of modern Glasgow as a microcosm of the human condition. Theirs is a city laden with the most extreme examples of the misery wrought by harsh working conditions, poor housing and widespread poverty. Unlike the noted Glasgow School of painters of the turn of the century, such as James Guthrie, Robert McGregor or E A Walton, in whose attempts at realism portrayals of the poor tended to be picturesque and sentimental, Currie and Howson employ instead the mode of representation of the German painters of the *Neue Sachlichkeit*. These young Scottish artists aim for an uncompromising realism, in which situations are presented with detailed and exaggerated forthrightness.

For Currie, a politically committed artist who comes close to the Mexican muralist Diego Rivera in articulating socialist ideology on a grand scale, the 'struggle' is paramount. Currie's agenda is clear; he makes art 'about working people, for working people . . .',[14] and he subscribes to the power of art to motivate people to improve their lot. Citing ignorance as a great impediment to progress, his engrossing, complex scenes portray members of the working classes involved in self-educational pursuits. A more despondent Currie appears as the worker/artist, tearing up his grand design for a better world, in a sequence from his *In the City Bar.*

Like Currie's paintings, Howson's hard-hitting unsentimental images are filled with the wretchedness and despair of Glasgow's poor. His subjects are young, musclebound toughs, engaged in 'masculine' activities – streetfighting, wrestling or football. Yet even though he abhors violence, Howson understands its origins. Glasgow's dossers – derelicts forced to sleep in cheap lodging houses – are the real heroes of Howson's low-life tragedies. Like the figure in *A Wing and a Prayer,* they assume heroic proportions and, though weighed down by the burden of constant hardships, they remain proud and defiant.

For Kevin Sinnott, tension is the common denominator of human relationships. Much of the uneasiness that pervades his imagery is derived from the situation itself, as he often portrays characters who are poised on the brink of some imminent confrontation. Sinnott depends upon stark lighting, stagey spatial rendering and exaggerated gesture to complement the drama contained within his paintings. Classical mythology is a particularly rich source for his thematic concerns and Baroque sensibility as in *Mother and Child,* based on the legend of the Sabine women.

Suzanne Treister's rich, seductive paintings are made up of improbable juxtapostions that can be both humorous and menacing. Treister uses the human heart as a surrogate for the actual figure because it is to her, 'the centre, both physical and emotional' of life.[15] In *Electric Chairs,* the arteries that emanate from the heart connect the human presence with the inanimate objects, the chairs, in the composition. But while these arteries function as conduits for the life force, they also contain an active electric current. Thus, the artist is proposing an allegory for our potential for self-destruction. She carries this notion further in *Detail of God's Underwear.* The electric drills which draw their source of power from the heart are overtly phallic symbols which Treister describes as 'instruments of potential violence; you don't really know what they are drilling into.'[16]

The point of Tim Head's image mutations is to reveal 'an artificial terrain of simulated textures and shapes in which, silently, anything can be changed into anything else'.[17] Thus, he seduces the viewer with tastefully designed patterns which, on closer inspection, turn out to be as banal as lamb chops, or as revolting as entrails. By reminding us that things are not always what they appear to be, however, Head intends not merely to raise questions about the fallibility of our perceptions. Rather, he addresses a larger concern for the way in which society has become the victim of the consumer culture it created. Not only are we reduced to products; we are, literally, what we eat. Environmental poisons, which threaten our interior mental and physical spaces, are most insidious when they come in pretty packages.

Graham Crowley addresses a multitude of contemporary

social issues in paintings of domestic life. While his interior scenes contain 'homey' conventions, such as brightly lit table lamps, Crowley's urban psychodramas are anything but comforting. The chaotic and squalid claustrophobia endured by city dwellers recalls the documentary and moralist tone of Charles Dickens, and the chilling prescience of George Orwell. Crowley unmasks obsessively pretentious notions of manners and decorum as hopelessly anachronistic in a modern setting. The house in *Peripheral Vision* is no longer a safe haven; its walls and doors, formerly barriers to evils that threaten its boundaries, are now reduced to rubble. The compressed, distorted spaces, and lurid effects of lighting are the visual equivalents of a nightmarish state of anxiety and despair.

The monumental, narrative paintings of Steven Campbell are complex in arcane detail, and rich in formal invention. Campbell draws upon a vast reserve of literary and illustrative sources, which intermingle with his imagination in fantastic scenarios ('I paint like someone who is trying to put as much as possible in.'[18]) Much of his imagery comes from his dual fascination with powerful myths and scientific or pseudo-scientific experiments. One popular myth which he persistently debunks in his paintings is that of a pastoral, rural England which ceased to exist long ago. Campbell shares this view of an Arcadian fiction and penchant for absurd happenings with P G Wodehouse, whose novels inspired the artist's paintings of Wee Nook. But Campbell's imagery conveys a mixture of humour and horror which Wodehouse never attempted. Campbell's world is one of terrifying situations and threatening environments which seem to to come together on some surreal stage. He exploits theatrical devices – dramatic poses and gestures, and landscapes serving as backdrops – retained from his days as a performance artist. As in *The Man who Gave his Legs to God and God Did not Want Them*, his lungeing characters seem to defy gravity as much as their predicaments defy logic.

Jonathan Waller's haunting *Sequel* proposes an epilogue to the ascendancy of the Industrial Age, heralded in Turner's 1844 masterpiece *Rain, Steam and Speed*. The abandoned, decaying locomotive, once the symbol of progress, is now reduced to a metaphor for a failed dream. Belly-up, it appears frozen in time like a petrified work horse. Waller's paintings of industrial archaeology owe a debt to 19th-century Romanticism both in the facture and approach to subject-matter. The material property of the paint is transformed into rust, while the warm ochre tonality evokes a mood that is more elegiac and wistful than disturbing.

If Sir Joshua Reynolds instructed the 18th-century Royal Academy's practitioners of the 'Grand Manner' of painting to restrict their subject-matter to references to poetry or the past, he would recognise his progeny *in extremis* as the contemporary history painter, Mark Wallinger. Wallinger lampoons the English national past by acknowledging the 'non-conformists' of the 18th and 19th centuries. In *Satire Sat Here* William Hogarth's image of the *Comic Muse* (a self-portrait in the act of painting) is relocated into opposing toilet bowls, which form both a visual palindrome and a mask. The reference to where 'Satire' sat places Hogarth in a context in which his socially critical art, as viewed by his contemporaries, would have been considered in very bad taste. Wallinger's *In the Hands of the Dilettanti* is borrowed from Sir Joshua's group portrait of the Society of the Dilettanti (who William Blake called 'Sir Sloshua and his gang of hired knaves'). Perched in the foreground is a toby-jug in the form of Blake's death mask. Blake takes on the role of both martyr and prophet in Wallinger's sad homage. Whether quoted in ironic, critical or subversive terms, Wallinger uses the past to comment on the present. The issue he addresses is, after all, the survival of British Painting.

Notes

1 The 'School of London' is the name given to this group of artists by the American-born R B Kitaj.
2 Quoted in Monica Bohm-Duchen, 'John Monks' *Flash Art* January/March 1986.
3 Ian McKeever and Thomas Joshua Cooper *The Staffa Project: A Collaboration* Harris Museum and Art Gallery, Preston 1987 p 44.
4 Interview by Matthew Collings, A*rtscribe* 46 May/July 1984 p 20.
5 Quoted in Patrick Kinmonth, 'Thérèse Oulton Painting' *British Vogue* July 1984.
6 Quoted in Caroline Collier, 'White Horses . . . Christopher Le Brun' *Studio International* Vol 192 No 1010 p 15.
7 *ibid* p 15.
8 Quoted in interview with Philip Vonn, 'Eileen Cooper: Painting from a Life' *Artist's and Illustrator's Magazine* September 1987 p 11.
9 *ibid* p 11.
10 Quoted by Andrew Graham-Dixon, 'Unquiet Mood' *British Vogue* February 1988 p 218.
11 *ibid* p 210.
12 Quoted in Alexander Moffat, *New Image Glasgow* Third Eye Centre Glasgow 1985 p 9.
13 Quoted in Robert Heller, *16 Artists' Process and Product* Angela Flowers Gallery London 1987.
14 Quoted in interview from information pack, 'In Touch with New Scottish Art', published in conjunction with *The Vigorous Imagination: New Scottish Art*, Scottish National Gallery of Modern Art Edinburgh 1987.
15 Interview with the artist, February 1988.
16 Interview with the artist, February 1988.
17 Quoted in Marina Vaizey, 'British Art Makes a Name for Itself' *The Sunday Times* 25 January 1987.
18 Quoted in interview from information pack, 'In Touch with New Scottish Art' *op cit.*

L to R: Simon Edmondson, *Elements*, 1986, oil; Jock McFadyen, *Rainy Day Women, L8*, 1986, oil

THERESE OULTON

Lachrimae, 1987, oil. Oulton's paintings, combining encrusted textures of interwoven, earthen pigments with titled references to alchemy and music, reveal a knowledge of art history, not in terms of surface quotations, but in the creative process itself. There is a sense of unresolved tension in her art, which recalls the traditional techniques of the 'old masters' and in particular the painting of Turner and Constable, meticulously applying and integrating coloured pigments through 'the chemistry of painting' to form a rich impasto, transforming the material processes of nature into an ambiguous painterly abstraction.

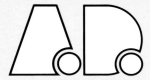

Art & Design
'The Art Magazine for the 80s'

Art & Design has quickly established a reputation for its influential, in-depth coverage of painting, sculpture and design. Always visually stunning, it takes its themes from current exhibitions or newly emergent trends, and gives its own fresh, thought-provoking angle on issues central to the art of today with articles by an international forum of critics, including Mary Rose Beaumont, Richard Cork, John Griffiths, Marco Livingstone and Robert Rosenblum.

An annual subscription for six double issues of *Art & Design*, including p&p, costs £35.00 in the UK, £39.50 in Europe, and US$75.00 or the sterling equivalent overseas.

A combined subscription for *Art & Design* and *Architectural Design*, giving six double issues of both magazines inclusive of p&p, is also available at the annual rate of £65.00 in the UK, £75.00 in Europe, and US$135.00 or the sterling equivalent overseas. On both the individual and combined subscriptions, students are entitled to a discount.

Individual issues can be ordered by mail for £7.95/US$19.95 + £1.00/US$3.00 (including p&p).

Recent and forthcoming issues:-

1/2-87	20th-Century British Art
3/4-87	The Post-Modern Object
5/6-87	Abstract Art
7/8-87	The Post-Avant-Garde
9/10-87	British & American Art
11/12-87	Sculpture Today
1/2-88	David Hockney
3/4-88	The New Modernism
5/6-88	The Classical Sensibility
7/8-88	Art in the Age of Pluralism
9/10-88	British Art Now
11/12-88	The New Romantics
1/2-89	Italian Art
3/4-89	40 Under 40
5/6-89	Malevich

Subscriptions Department
ACADEMY GROUP LTD
7/8 Holland Street
London W8 4NA
Tel: 01-402 2141

All major credit cards accepted

ART & DESIGN MAGAZINE SUBSCRIPTION

Please send me one year's subscription to Art & Design

Full rate UK £35.00 Europe £39.50 Overseas US$75.00 Students UK £29.50 Europe £34.00 Overseas US$65.00

☐ **Payment enclosed by cheque/postal order/draft**

☐ **Please charge £ . . . . . to my credit card account no:**

Expiry date . . . .

Signature ....

Name ....

Address..

....

....

Subscriptions Department
ACADEMY GROUP LTD
7/8 Holland Street
LONDON W8 4NA

ARCHITECTURAL DESIGN + ART & DESIGN

Please send me one year's subscription to both magazines

Special introductory combined rate UK £65.00 Europe £75.00 Overseas US$135.00
Special introductory student rate UK £59.50 Europe £69.50 Overseas US$120.00

☐ **Payment enclosed by cheque/postal order/draft**

☐ **Please charge £ . . . . . to my credit card account no:**

Expiry date . . . .

Signature ....

Name ....

Address..

....

....

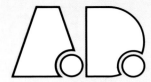

Architectural Design

Architectural Design continues its tradition of vigorous and wide-ranging treatment of architectural trends of vital importance to today. The issues, which are published six times a year on alternate months, are each devoted to a major theme of topical relevance. Leading architects to be featured in 1989 include Peter Eisenman, Michael Graves, Zaha Hadid, Hans Hollein, Arata Isozaki, Charles Jencks, Leon Krier, Daniel Libeskind, Richard Meier, Cesar Pelli, Aldo Rossi, Denise Scott Brown, James Stirling, Bernard Tschumi and SITE.

An annual subscription for *Architectural Design*, including postage and packing, costs £45.00 in the UK, £55.00 in Europe, US$99.50 or the sterling equivalent overseas.

A combined subscription for *Architectural Design* and *Art & Design*, giving six double issues of both magazines inclusive of postage and packing, is also available at the special introductory annual rate of £65.00 in the UK, £75.00 in Europe, and US$135.00 or the sterling equivalent overseas.

For both the individual and combined subscriptions, students are entitled to a discount.

Individual issues can be ordered by mail at a cost of £7.95/US$19.95 + £1.00/US$3.00 postage and packing per issue.

Please complete the subscription form opposite and send it with your payment
NOW

All major credit cards accepted

KAREN FORSYTH

L to R: Bacchus in his Dressing Gown, 1988, oil; *The Fall of Icarus*, 1988, oil. Karen Forsyth's swirling melodramas are inspired by Classical mythology, Baroque ceilings and Viennese opera. *The Fall of Icarus* (a particularly popular theme for young artists in the 80s) is perhaps a moral warning to all those who assume too much or aim too high.

LOUISE BLAIR

L to R: The Watchful, 1988; *Immortality*, 1988, both oil on linen, Louise Blair's work draws its ambiguous symbolism from a variety of sources. Her recent paintings contain strong landscape and natural elements but also retain some of the quasi-religious figures of her earlier 'portrait' works, as in the shadowy figures looking out to sea in *The Watchful*, other elements suggest cliffs and rocks. In *Immortality* lilies, a stormy sky, architectural details perhaps of a church combine to create a vivid personal scene.

Heaven and Hell (after Leonardo's *Deluge*), 1989, oil

STEPHEN FARTHING

In England, if you wear a long face, people will think you are serious; and if they think you are serious, as David Bailey recently pointed out to Melvyn Bragg, they will think you are talented. Stephen Farthing, as far as I know, has never worn a long face; in life I associate him with laughter and off-the-cuff jokes, with zest in other words; and zestfulness – in a single word – has surely come to be the over-riding character of his paintings: they are invigorating, bursting with sensual vim and intellectual vigour, and emotionally complete – never so dark that they cannot be witty, never so witty that they cannot be dark.

In this they emphasise, they revel in, the one advantage painting has over the other arts; an advantage Gauguin pinpointed:

Painting is the most beautiful of all the arts. In it, sensation is concentrated; before it, everyone is free to imagine what they will, without the burden of having to remember anything, everything being already there . . . Like literature, the art of painting tells whatever it wants, with the advantage of letting the reader immediately know the prelude, the story and the epilogue.

And there is something else he said which seems pertinent to Farthing's attitude: 'Go on working, *freely and furiously* . . . Above all, don't sweat over a picture. Feeling can be expressed instantaneously.'

If Farthing has agonised over a painting – and what artist doesn't – it never shows. Nor has he ever been stumped for an idea. One of his most singular gifts is his adaptability. He has always made paintings which have benefitted from and been affected by his surroundings and circumstances. This has been as true of his variations on some royal portraits at Versailles, seen during a term's sabbatical in Paris as a student in 1975, as of his recent speculations on aerial warfare and home comforts in Farnham, where he is currently Head of Painting at West Surrey College of Art and Design. Now he has just completed another sabbatical spring term, this time as the Hayward Gallery's first artist-in-residence, the appointment designed to coincide with the Leonardo exhibition. Farthing is a painter who teaches, not a teacher who paints.

This adaptability made him an inspired choice. An artist of a less-inquiring mind might reasonably have baulked at Leonardo. But for Farthing the project teemed with possibilities. Visiting his orange portakabin on one of the Hayward's windy flight-decks three weeks after the opening, I found him working 'freely' and intricately (as well as 'furiously') on four large canvases. 'Leonardo da Vinci is so eminently conservative and respectable', I had read in *The Times* on the day of my visit; a quick tour of the show in Farthing's company soon dispelled such complacent assumptions. At the time Farthing was particularly enthusiastic about drawing No 65, *A Cloudburst of Material Possessions*, showing pots, pans, rakes and God-knows-what other rubbish raining down from some clouds. It only added to the fun that the catalogue caption to this scene reads: 'It is not easy to tell what is happening in this extraordinary drawing . . .' – the cataloguer should try walking under more ladders in future.

Beyond his pleasure in the wit and novelty of this image Farthing considers it an auto-biographical piece, a metaphor of the master's own state of mind – a jovial, maybe rueful, acknowledgement of his bursting imagination, an imagination which made him notoriously bad at finishing things. Even on a single sheet Leonardo can wander off the point. No 77 shows a study for the National Gallery's recently mutilated cartoon of *The Virgin and Child with St Anne and the Infant John the Baptist*, but in the margins there are doodles of a baby, a wrestling couple, water-wheels and dams. This proved another favourite with Farthing, because of the insight it offers into Leonardo's method. But it was the famous *Deluge* drawings from which he was deriving the most in his first canvases.

On a recent visit to France he had been captivated by an old mural showing an aerial perspective view of the château in which he was standing; and at the Hayward he initially envisaged a three-dimensional model of one of Leonardo's *Deluge* drawings standing in front of a similar image; a jovial reference to the didactic aspects of the installation. But on canvas he realised that the image would be far more intense if the two images were seen to exist on equal terms, a 'real' city (he eventually chose Florence) threatened by a 'real' deluge. Provisionally he entitled the variations on this theme, *Heaven and Hell*, though he does not consider the paintings to be allegories:

The Florence flood did cross my mind; but for me they are much more a celebration of drawing and painting. How do you bring a drawing into a painting? How do you make one thing re-emerge as something else? I have never made drawing such an issue in a painting.

If Leonardo's superb hand has one ruling graphic character it might be described as 'thoughtfulness' – not a very 20th-century graphic quality; so it is a nice conceit that Farthing's scrupulous drawing of the city should be achieved with a fine air-brush – a quintessential piece of 20th-century graphic equipment. From this juxtaposition of map-making precision and free-expression, of the rational and the irrational, Farthing proceeds to build 'castles in the air' to tower over the intricacies of Florence, like the triumph of the mind over matter.

It is this vitality and purpose that distinguish his painting from the contemporary flux, in which banal and arbitrary quotation so often poses as knowledge, slapstick and sensation as energy. Farthing is to be one of the British contingent at this year's Sao Paulo Biennale in October, and thinks he may choose to be represented by the Leonardo cycle. It will make a stunning show and no doubt help to establish the international reputation he so richly deserves.

John McEwen

L to R: Sistina, 1977-8, mixed media; *Seen As*, 1987, oil

JOHN KEANE

L to R: The Chorus, 1988, oil; *Blips*, 1988, oil. Combining expressionistic brushstrokes with graffiti-like scrawls to survey British politics and society, the worker and his accoutrements, Keane's light-hearted imagery – the featureless faces of *The Chorus*, where lives are dominated by the supermarket trolley and the lawnmower, and the figure in *Blips* blindfolded to battleship and nuclear missiles – brings out, rather than harsh political dogmatism, the folly and ignorance of the ordinary anonymous man.

KEN CURRIE

Life Grows Hard, 1988, oil. 'I felt that my new commitments lay in the realities of today and my own urban experiences . . . I have to maintain a dialectical tension between positive and negative aspects of the world in order to pursue both a critical and visionary realism . . . my aim, in the end, is to paint about the realities of the human condition as well as to depict the existing possibilities for world reconstruction.'

PAUL STOREY

Isotta, 1986, oil. Based on the legend of Tristan and Isolde, this is one of Storey's most complex compositions. Although his works show affinities with contemporary Classicist painters such as Balthus, the strongest influence is the Early Renaissance – the static figures, the gestures and colours, the barren rocky landscape, the references to time and sexuality; but the rules and symbols of perspective, with hints of Uccello and an Orcagna Day of Judgement, are disjointed and disrupted in a 20th-century confusion.

KEITH MCINTYRE

 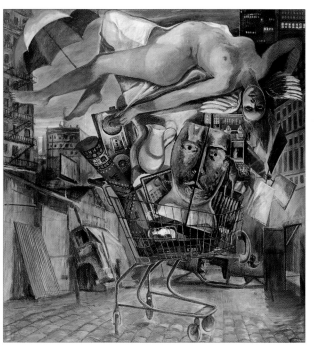

L to R: *Our Worldly Possessions*, 1988, oil; *The Story so Far – An Exercise in Nostalgia*, 1988, oil. McIntyre's recent paintings continue to reveal his knowledge of art history, creating a sense of spatial confusion through the forced coexistence of mythical figures and animals, references to the arts, and mass-produced objects such as tape-recorders and shopping trolleys. The titles comment on the nature of a mass consumer culture that seeks to temper the sense of discontinuity by looking back to the past.

SONIA BOYCE

The contextualising of self and identity are grounded in issues of culture, race, gender, sexuality, class and history. It might sound like quite a heavy task to begin at such a broad sea of concerns. Obviously I don't calculate, employ or am not fully conscious of all these concerns at once, but I try to find possible media as containers, drawing on the relationship of these issues to personal experiences. This year I have been looking back at the work I have done: what appears as a common link is migration, of people migrating from one place to another, and what happens at the point of meeting, the place they came from and the place they go to.

Because of the way that the different Black (African, Afro-Caribbean and Asian) communities in Britain have had to fight for basic space, what has emerged is a strong sense of community. With this has come a cheering expectation that individuals of the Black community in the public gaze should be delegates or representatives of the community. As a visual artist I have continual battles when making work between self and identity (social structures) and representation (depiction/delegation). There is a certain pressure to speak for or talk about a 'homogeneous' community which, of course, we are not. At the same time there is a need not only to make ourselves visible but also to explore our reflections, in a multitude of ways. Whether as individuals or bringing together our common experiences.

I want to make work that explores my, and in turn my generation's, relationship to our parents and their cultural background and how we negotiate living here in Britain as a second generation. To put it another way, information that our parents pass on to us about cultural and spiritual aspects of their lives in the Caribbean that we don't have a full sense of. Understanding only fragments. Again I rely on personal experiences, particularly in the arena of the family, to expose pertinent issues. One of the results of drawing on the many fragments of identity and self, coupled with trying to develop an alternative visual language to the dominant culture, is the conflict of subject matter and the conveying object. I write notes and list things and sometimes the image and the words come together. Sometimes a title comes before the image. But it is not very often that the image comes before sorting out the ideas. I think it is a habit specific to the way in which at art college I had to talk to defend what I was doing. I had to be responsible for everything I made. Through groups of ideas rather than groups of work a rhythm emerges.

I do plan a series of work but it always seems to culminate in two or three pieces.

This year [1988] I have been trying to rethink my responsibility as an image maker. That responsibility, in terms of representation and dispelling the existing stereotypes, can be quite restrictive. I am trying to allow myself space to make things that could be dangerous in what the works might say. My interest in the deconstruction of visual language comes out of an involvement with the Feminist Art movement. Again in terms of developing an alternative language, where can you look to find appropriate images? I guess this is one of the reasons my family and I feature strongly in the work. Explaining or even understanding why sexuality, the use of nature (fish, leaves, birds etc), invitation and a sense of claustrophobia are recurring vehicles for discussing ongoing themes is difficult. Obviously they are important, but it is hard to see the reasons for that. Making objects has been a way of exorcising aspects of myself and particular experiences, some of which are negative. I suppose that is where my sense of dangerous territory lies. How far can I push those representations and where will it take it me?

Sonia Boyce

Talking Presence, 1988, mixed media on photographic paper

GRAHAM DEAN

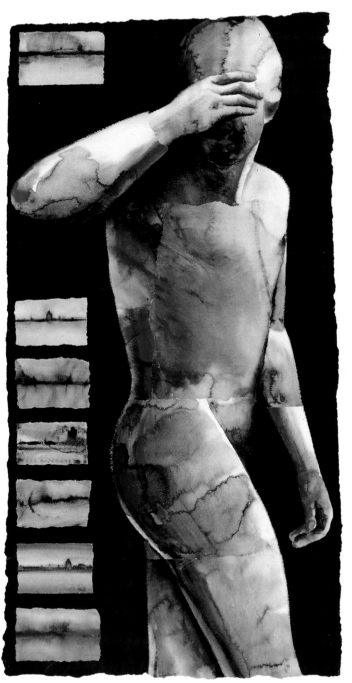

Above L: *The Kiss*, 1987, watercolour and acrylic; *Below L*: *Foreign Correspondent*, 1987, watercolour; *Right*: *Legacy*, 1987-8, watercolour. 'Each picture comprises of several parts which are torn into place after I have painted them, ie, one sheet of paper might be a leg, another a torso, another an arm, etc. This often results in odd juxtapositions which can be manipulated, and, as a consequence I will start a picture with only an outline knowledge as to its development and size . . . I like to see these works as having a combination of strength and vulnerability. I relish the subtlety of watercolour, but my aim is to combine this with those strengths normally associated with being a painter rather than a watercolourist.'

MADELEINE STRINDBERG

'Within each painting I am trying to find an image that reflects a specific emotion with the highest possible psychological charge, an essence of being alive with an ever present awareness of its impermanence and fragility.' That rather ambitious statement is taped to the wall just inside the door of the temporary studio in the National Gallery, at present occupied by Madeleine Strindberg, the ninth and last artist to hold the post of Artist-in-Residence at the National Gallery in its current format. Discussions as to how the scheme is to develop are currently underway, but the Gallery remains committed to actively involving practising artists in a manner that will mean that both they and their work will be accessible to the public.

The scheme was initiated in 1979, when Maggi Hambling was invited to become the first incumbent, and since then the postholder has been selected by open competition, including studio visits and interviews. A list of past artists includes Michael Porter, Jock McFadyen, Hughie O'Donoghue and June Redfern, all of whom opened their National Gallery studio on a Friday afternoon, to a public whose response varied from the predictable 'my five year old could do better', to the enthusiastic, intrigued and supportive.

Strindberg studied at the Byam Shaw School of Art and at the Royal College of Art. In 1985, she was joint winner of the Barclay Prize with work which revealed tremendous technical accomplishment. Since then her work has almost consciously turned its back on the initially impressive or visually attractive, resulting in a series of particularly uncompromising paintings. 'The pretty, seductive things have got to go, if they don't have meaning', she says.

The visitor to Strindberg's studio is confronted with a paint-spattered floor, stacks of huge canvases against the walls, and one or two works in progress. Taped apparently at random to the walls are small paintings on paper, which exist primarily as small-scale experiments, as things which will maybe trigger off ideas in the large paintings. Although these small works are often of great delicacy and beauty, to Strindberg scale is of the utmost importance: 'The content of my work demands monumentality – partly to avoid notions of domesticity and safety. It is important that the painting suggests a world one can physically enter, that surrounds you, that can be felt with every gesture or mark.'

The initial months of the residence proved somewhat difficult. The upheaval of leaving her own studio for the studio in the National Gallery, long-standing teaching commitments, and the continual pressure of having to meet the public every week all contributed to a reinforced reassessment and questioning of values. Finding herself every Friday in a situation of having to 'defend' and explain the not yet completed, could at times be destructive and disorientating. This, however, was eventually outweighed by an unexpected engagement by members of the public with the work – a willingness to understand and learn, which at times resulted in unexpected involvement and enthusiasm.

It is therefore these Friday sessions with the public that previous Artists-in-Residence look back on as having been of particular benefit, even if it had not seemed so at the time. Obviously, from the Gallery's point of view, part of the purpose of the scheme is to show how art did not suddenly stop around 1900, but is a continuously evolving process and that the National Gallery's collection is relevant to artists working today. More subtly, the scheme also acts as a gentle reminder that the old canvases on the main floor, in their heavy gilded frames, all originate from artists' studios and workshops, and that they were all made by human beings.

But from the artist's point of view, it is meeting the public, and the responses from that public that provides a vital contact with a 'non-professional' world. Many of her visitors are art students and amateur artists, drawn to the Gallery by the presence of a living artist. 'Art is essentially born out of solitude, isolation and reflection – to be forced into exposure and communication on a weekly basis can be extremely challenging and demanding.'

A more immediately obvious bonus is, of course, the opportunity of working for six months in the heart of one of the finest collections of old masters in the world. It has not been part of the artist's brief to work directly from the collection by way of making transcriptions, although, for example, both Maggi Hambling and Michael Porter did this out of choice. For Strindberg though, the collection exists more as an inspiration and catalyst, rather than as something to take direct ideas from. The large-scale Baroque drama of Luca Giordano's *Followers of Phineas Turned to Stone* is a particular favourite. 'Somehow I feel I shouldn't really like it' she says, 'but I do. Then there is always Rembrandt's simplicity and essence. It is those qualities I hope to capture in my own work.'

Colin Wiggins

Resurrection, triptych, oil

I am concerned with making paintings that deal with images that express psychological states and inner realities. They are not referential to the seen, but based on my own internal experiences and feelings, my own inner being. I see my work as an inner centre, an extension of the self. The forms and colours I am using are there for specific, metaphorical and symbolic reasons, never on purely visual grounds, and never descriptive or narrative of a seen reality. The subject matter is referential to the human body, specifically to what it is like being a woman. The aim is clarity, the specific rather than the general, confrontational to the point of rawness/the absurd. The process has recently taken two different leads:

Above L to R: Infliction, 1988, oil. *Within*, 1988, oil; The 'organic', 'fluent' paintings. Born out of the process, unpremeditated and unpredictable, attempting to catch the moment where recognition frees the image, awareness disentangles chaos and physical sensation take on a visual presence. Dealing with the illusion of control, versus ultimate fragility. Large black shapes being the protagonists of the drama, concealing the human being, revealing the emotion.

Below L to R: Cross, 1988, oil and metal; *Center*, 1988, oil and metal. The 'metal' paintings. Large sheets of metal, fixed to the canvas used for its properties of semi-reflectiveness, lack of flexibility, lack of compromise. Being sheer matter hence destroying any possibility of illusion. Dealing with a tangible reality, the here and now, – hard, cold and unyielding – embedded, sunk into lush velvety soft black. Infinite, dark and relentless. **Madeleine Strindberg**

LANCE SMITH

To look at the work of Lance Smith is to look also at the world in which we live. If the 'Doomsday Clock' is a little less likely to strike midnight, ecological disaster seems destined to slowly erode our environment and survival hangs, as ever, by its precarious thread. If we don't need reminding, we do perhaps need to know that others share our doubts and anxieties. Lance Smith's painting does just that.

There is, however, another side to Smith's work. The paintings present us with a richly encrusted patina, a tactile quality that is both positive and life affirming in its material presence. The paintings seem to invite our touch and certainly bear witness to the physical contact of the artist. Smith was originally trained as a sculptor, as his working practice constantly reminds us. A sculptural sensitivity arises, not only from the physical abrasions of the surface, but also from the sparing use of colour, which rarely strays from the sombre greys of granite or the verdigris of weathered bronze. The suggestion of crudely drawn profiles has more in common, too, with the sculptor's chisel, than the painter's more delicate tools.

Although narrative, the work is far from illustrative. Smith often works in series and when works of a similar genesis are hung together a sequential narrative emerges. These themes (I hesitate to call them motifs) are drawn from a variety of sources, but whether Classical or reflecting contemporary events, they serve as a universal metaphor. Thus the *Icarus*, *Requiem*, *Divide*, *Dispossessed* and *Fall* series each evoke feelings of isolation and unease, of a searching for identity, or of a sense of impending disaster.

The earlier works dealt more exclusively with individual and often autobiographical references, but recently Smith has refused to be tied down to specifics. His work is now less responsive to actual events and more open to a generalised reading. In the process he has become less dependent on drawing, and the staccato figures, while still implicit, are no longer sketched on to the picture plane. In abandoning specific narrative means the recent paintings do not surrender their secrets with the ease that we have come to expect in the 1980s. It is one of Smith's great strengths that the work should demand time and the active involvement of the viewer, for such demands are inherent to themes which themselves do not lead to easy solutions. Thus, Smith's paintings often verge on the chaotic, where the energy is not constrained by a need for formal harmony or balance, and the final act of resolution is left to the spectator. There is an obvious risk which the artist accepts, but when successful the observer is drawn into the creative act, while the paintings maintain the full force of an unfettered dynamism. I once described Smith's work as being just short of *meltdown*, the point at which both the formal and spiritual energy threaten to break loose the restraints of picture making.

Colour, or more precisely its absence, also plays an important role. Unlike many of the younger generation who mistake a cacophany of hues for the expression of feeling, Smith's almost monochrome canvases have a base and earthy resonance. The alchemy of collaged material, scoured surfaces and earth pigments brings Smith close to much European painting, particularly the work of the contemporary Spanish artist Antoni Tàpies or the German Anselm Kiefer. This European (rather than International) identity imbues the work with a sense of belonging, its roots feeling their way back towards an older culture.

The awareness of his relationship to past masters is certainly another source of Smith's strength. The force and directness of Bacon or of Goya's *Black Paintings* is often apparent and so too, I believe, is the debt owed to Romanticism. The identification with a tradition which takes the figure, or figure in the landscape, as a potent metaphor for Man's spiritual searching is crucial. Although the formal innovations of shallow space and surface mark owe much to the later 20th century, the spirit of the work is closer to the Great Masters than to the austere and inward looking cannons of Modernism.

It is surprising to realise that Smith's career as a painter has been remarkably short. Graduating from the Royal Academy in 1976, the transition from sculpture to painting was long and arduous. Arguably, this gestation period (and the absence of a formal training in painting) has worked to the artist's advantage. *The Iconoclast*, Smith's first truly mature painting, won the Tolly Cobbold Award in 1985. Two solo exhibitions followed at the Fabian Carlsson Gallery, with a one man showing at Bristol's Arnolfini, and a five venue British tour in 1988. Having shown at Forum, Zurich the previous year, Smith also won a gold medal at the 2nd Baghdad International Festival, competing with over 400 artists from 40 countries. The work will receive further international exposure with a Madrid showing planned for later in 1989.

Despite this impressive record, and participating in a number of group shows, Smith has yet to be included in any definitive surveys. The reason is all too obvious, for Smith's work sits uneasily alongside the gaily coloured pastiches of New Figuration. It is unfortunate that our first inclination is to measure work by its peers. Seen from another perspective, perhaps in the context of the School of London figuration, Smith's work could be seen both as a strong, individual voice and as one which belongs firmly within the tradition of European painting.

Keith Patrick

L to R: Big Divide, 1988-9, oil and acrylic; *Hell and High Water (after Uccello) Part I* and *Part II*, 1988, mixed media

JONATHAN WALLER

Above: *End of the Line*, 1987, oil; *Below*: *Break-Down*, 1986, oil. Symbolic decaying machines, romanticised visions of wasteland, rusting cogs redolent with nostalgia and titles such as *End of the Line*, *Degeneration*, *Break-Down*; a few especially the more recent works contain figures – idealised visions of the trusty worker or craftsman – but it is the machines that dominate Waller's paintings. What lifts them above the mechanical or mundane is the fluency of handling and the subtle use of colour within a restricted, often near monochrome range. As well as large oils on canvas he does small expressive studies in ink and pastel or recent experimentations with waterbased paints and varnish.

ANDREW CARNIE

A World of Possibilities

The most recurrent aspect of my work during the past eight years has been the use of three-dimensional sculpture built into a painterly format. It's that area that most people are drawn to in my work and I think it is where most of my inventiveness has occurred, trying to explore it with a sense of humour that belies its serious intent. Why I developed work in this area I'm never quite sure. I think in the main, it was through a period of object-making, that I undertook while at college. I decided making things in the workshops allowed me to complete a work without disturbing criticism. (Painting always seemed a particularly private activity.) The object and its parts were very much there, not imagined, the completion of a work was a clear act. After this period of almost two years, which had been a period of repression of painting, I still badly wanted to paint, so I began to incorporate these objects into the paintings. The concrete objects allowed a safe starting place for the painting that followed.

Of course, there were precedents for this type of work. In early days, I drew on the works of Jasper Johns, Rauschenberg and Jim Dine. Later, Robert Longo, Paladino and David Salle became important influences. The work also infused ideas from Minimalist artists like Joel Shapiro whose work had affected the general art atmosphere and my early objects. These influences were blended together with everyday observations and surprising influences from the past – religious polychrome sculpture from northwest Spain, formal devices from early Italian works, like the Cimabue crucifix. All these sources brought forth elements, which were to affect the different ways I have investigated the painting/sculpture boundary. Always though, I think of them as paintings first, and never the other way around.

In one series of my works, the sculptural elements are continuations of the canvas itself. Though made of wood, card or foam, or cast in fibreglass, the objects are covered with a patchwork of canvas; the whole being primed and treated like a normal canvas. So in *Coming and Going*, 1983, the suitcase becomes an extension of the canvas surface, blended into it before the images of destinations in Europe were painted. In *Observation*, 1982, the sculptured form is less attached: a box and five cylinders, one on each exposed side, all canvas covered, form a satellite which floats above a map. The box is painted to represent a case of Heinz products, and the cylinders become Coke cans. A jokey corporate sputnik looks ominously down. Sometimes real objects like keys or coat hooks erupt from the surface. On larger works, 'real' takes the form of old cans, labelling still apparent, pop-riveted together, to make forms like ski-lifts, or awned walkways, projecting from the canvas surface.

In all these pieces, the three-dimensional sections act as intriguing ways into the paintings. They rest between the two-dimensional painting and the real world, making a link between reality and the tenuous world of dream and imagination. They bridge the gap and also serve as 'enablers', allowing an exploration of painting. In the 60s and 70s, painting seemed almost taboo. Our minds were manicled to a state of 'do not paint'. For me, in the early 80s, incorporating objects into paintings allowed an engagement with a domain of art that had been neglected, overlooked and highly criticised. It was a backdoor to our more 'pluralistic order' today, where minimalism, figuration and expressionism stand side-by-side. The sculptural aspect, which was then a more acceptable medium, allowed me to come to terms with oil paint. The versatility of oil paint to make any image is its most endearing quality and also the most difficult element to control. The sculptural element not only allowed me to begin to use oil paint, but also acted as an anchor or qualitative reference point for the painting that followed.

My largest works consist of two panels joined by a figure which bisects them. The figure is developed as the sculptural element, at times completely framed by the surrounding canvas, (*Eyes*, 1987); at other times extending the piece into the gallery as in *Downs*, 1986, where a 'Moore-like' figure sits with his feet on the gallery floor, interacting with onlookers, while his back rests against a painted landscape scene, his arms along the panel tops. Landscape and aerial views have featured extensively in this type of work, but elsewhere, images with reference to travel and escape seem prevalent. These are often set against household objects real or painted. The image used, very much depends on my preoccupations at a particular time. For example, hammer images may occur when I have been re-structuring the studio.

The piece *Hammers*, 1983, exemplifies another type of work. The 'hammers', made of vacu-forms covered with canvas and painted, agitate in a suspended plane, across a painting of a willow-patterned china cup. This belongs to a series of work, where I have tried to extend the painting format, by adding another layer or screen to the work. Different activities go on above the canvas surface, sometimes relating to what is below, sometimes not. It is almost like looking into an archaeological dig with events uncovered from different ages. In other pieces 'pocket watches' move across the continent of Africa, or match-made men fly in front of a gigantic hand holding the box from where they originate. An alchemical change has taken place in form and mind.

For many areas of my work, 'experimentation' is the by-word. In a family of works made for the Angela Flowers Gallery, called *Vista*, 1988, the shape of the stretchers produced the sculptural component. Forms were added to the sides of rectangular canvases, before the actual imagery was conceived. This allowed an exciting interaction between form and content as the images developed, producing odd juxtapositions and conflicts in some works. The form did not always determine the image as in *Observation* from 1983. Spirals become flat pathways, interacting with added forest scenes, or in *Girls' Talk*, 1987, a coiled form ominously waits outside the painted square, unravelling the image, or waiting to spring. Boundaries are smudged, physical forms or bodies are animated by contrary images. This is likened to minds being constrained by their physical form. In some cases mind, or image, seemed to conquer the matter or form. In other works the reverse was true.

Not all the work has been confined to this cross between sculpture and painting. Sometimes I have ventured into photography, in pieces like *Pause*, 1986, or *Swing*, 1988, and a body of pure painting and sculpture exists. Here, the qualities of differing disciplines do not intermingle. In shows, these different types of work are often placed together in complex environment settings or installations. This has been true from the very first show at Goldsmiths in 1982, through to the most recent exhibition *Under Canvas*, 1988 at the Giray Gallery, London. Here, the sculpture and paintings fell into separate categories, but even so, some cross-references were evident. Two of the sculptures were made from a large number of painted canvas stretchers, (*Pill Box*, 1988), while the paintings were of sculptural forms made of these same basic building blocks, (*Retreat*, 1988). Even in this latest installation canvas and paint have been given one more possibility, but here the work is touched by 'fear' more than the early exuberance. The artist is seen as being on the defensive – the painting has become the barricade, as in *Tide*, 1988, and, as in *Raft*, 1988, the studio is now the place to dream.

Andrew Carnie

Above L to R: Retreat, 1988, oil; *Observation*, 1982, oil, box, cylinders; *Below L to R: Flight*, 1986; *Downs*, 1986, both oil and painted metal

MARK WALLINGER

Above: *Passport Control*, 1988, colour photographs installation; *Below*: *Satire Sat Here*, 1986, oil. Wallinger comments on the present by quoting from art history in ironic, often subversive terms. In *Passport Control*, he assembles mass-produced passport photographs – self-portraits in disguise – which question the notions of identity (both artistic and cultural) and self-creation (or manipulation), commenting on contemporary issues and undermining the concept of the self-portrait in art history. Self-creation is again explored in *Satire Sat Here* in which a quotation from Hogarth is subverted, and the painting transformed into a mask.

British Künst, 1988,

gouache on paper, triptych

DAVID MACH

Above: *The Art That Came Apart*, Montreal, 1988, mixed media; *Below*: *Tamed Trained Framed*, Brussels, 1989, mixed media. David Mach is known for his technique of stacking and weaving everyday components such as magazines, transforming repetitive, mundane objects into instantly recognisable depictions of familiar things, in an attempt to break down the boundaries between art and life. In his recent installations, Mach takes his ideas a step further, assembling mass-produced, transient objects which retain their own identity, working co-operatively to entertain, to communicate on a level of common recognition and to provoke thought. Above all he aims to make his ideas accessible to those who might not normally look at art, breaking down distinctions between fine art and popular culture, and forcing new awareness of consumer waste and the transient nature of contemporary society.

HELEN CHADWICK

Helen Chadwick is engaged in an autobiography. Her subject is herself. She is renowned for the diversity and originality of her media; she has employed three-dimensional sculptural forms, the photocopying machine, the camera, light projections, and most recently the microscope and the computer. This inventiveness should not distract from the course of the work itself, which is a persistent exploration of *self*. The process is one of argument with her own reflection. Unlike a photographer, a category into which she is too easily placed by systematic curatorial minds, she creates sculptural forms of her own image or employs metaphors of tactile suggestion. Her recurring dilemma is one of separation, as if by a membrane, from her own reflection. Her imagery extends beyond the two dimensions of the photographic print and she frequently stages her art within the theatrical conventions of an installation. Then, as if to denounce the tangibility of the membrane, she has used light to project the image, so that both herself and her depicted counterpart are retained in an ephemeral, transient, realm, defined by this invisible membrane.

The vocabulary of her personal history takes on history itself. She has a direct, personal root in Athens, which heightens her sense of the Classical order underlying the geometry we all inhabit. Her first structures were created out of pure geometrical form, on to which was printed the membrane of the self-image. Photography is inescapably *of the moment*, the medium of the everlasting present. She is engaged in some personal archaeology in which she has photographed her past. She has conjured memory of herself at an age before even memory was part of her consciousness. *Ego Geometria Sum*, 1982-4, was introduced by her statement, 'Suppose one's body could be traced through a succession of geometric solids, as rare and pure as crystalline structures. . . then let this model of mathematical harmony be infused with a poetry of feeling and memory to sublimate the discord of past passion and desire in a recomposed neutrality of being.' Beginning with the incubator and ending with a full statuesque figure, she created ten geometrical forms on to which she printed her own evolving form.

Transience, the state of flux, became the force with which she challenged a finite world, the Newtonian heritage. In contrast to pure line and Classical order, she embraced chaos and decay. *Of Mutability*, 1984-6, her most ambitious installation, involved the literal decay of organic matter. She created a dark ocean of animal and plant form, in which her own naked body swam and cavorted in sensual exuberance, amidst maggots, flesh and organs. This visceral descent was depicted on a huge scale using the photocopier. She decked her body in frills and trimmings to further heighten the transience in contrast to the permanence implied by solidity and austerity. At the same time she found excitement in the elaboration of Rococo and Baroque architecture in which geometrical order was overladen with an effusion of decoration. She then surrounded *The Oval Court*, her sea of decay from *Of Mutability*, with Salamonic Columns created on a computer and derived from the Baldachino in St Peter's in Rome. She framed her chaos in architectural structure of the most ornate character.

Following a visit in 1987 to the paintings in the caves of Perigord, she saw the bridge between prehistory and the present manifest under the flickering light of a candle. She was then attracted to light as the literal form of her next work. In *Lofos Nymphon*, 1987, she returned to Athens and her mother. The return was the perfect coincidence. She re-employed the iconography of the mother and child against a backdrop of Athens itself on a sequence of five egg-shaped panels joined by a single line, like the line of a personal history and the line of her culture springing from the source of the city. The work was an attempt to re-locate the centre of the circle in which herself had been circumscribed, like a search for the missing navel of the ancient world and her true history.

She has now furthered the descent, past the surface of the body, the skin reflected in her self-image, through the viscera and into the body tissue. This preoccupation with stretching the finite boundaries of self and its depiction leads towards the structure of cells and the revelations of microbiology. The cell, like the atom, was once a finite unit, a scientific full stop, and is now a mass of further particles beyond the nucleus, just as electrons invisibly constitute the structure of the atom, and the single unit has become a multiple being. Passing from the jargon of the technological revolution, through the jargon of the media revolution, we enter the age of the biological revolution, where we are at war with the virus. Taking her body tissue, she has mixed her cells with the coastline via computer in a sequence of five great *Viral Landscapes*, 1988-9. In a single moment she is both microscopic and macroscopic. We see the edge of the body of the land, its rolling, feminine contours stroked by the sea. The landscape is no longer an inert subject for Romantic illustration. It becomes an active being subject to ravagement. When mixed with the colour of the cellular world, the land appears wrapped as if in embryonic waters. As she advances through the medium of science, she reasserts the presence of the land with all the animism of an ancient, primary imagination. The computer fuses her image with our common world. As her work continues in this pursuit of the elusive self, we might start to recognise our own multiple reflections.

Mark Holborn

Three Houses: A Modern Moral Subject, 1987, slide projections on to painted wall, installation at Hayward Gallery

WILLIE DOHERTY

Above: *Dreaming, Derry*, 1987; *Below*: *Fog, Ice, Derry*, 1985, both photograph with text. 'One of the issues that I obviously got involved in through using black and white photography, was its history and the history of how Derry was documented. However part of my strategy in using colour is to actually heighten the sense of artificiality of the photographic image. It is perhaps one of its paradoxes that, through appearing more real, it actually increases the sense of it being artificial . . . In the 70s there was an established form, a way in which works that used photograph and text looked, to some extent my work mimics that, but my use of that is ironic.'

NEW IRISH ART
From Recent Exhibitions

Above L to R: Wilson, *Interior World*, 1987, mixed media; Donnelly, *Donkey with Easter Lilies*, 1988, oil;
Below L to R: Coombes, *Riddle of the Cinematic World*, 1986, charcoal; Mulcahy, *Gate Ways I*, 1987, oil

The rise of a number of interesting young Irish artists has not gone unnoticed by the international exhibition circuit and gives us the opportunity to present here some of those artists who have recently been exhibited. As well as solo shows, several recent group exhibitions in Britain, Ireland and on the Continent have presented the work of Irish artists, the most ambitious of these being the exhibition *Irland-Deutschland Exchange* showing the work of 14 artists from either side of the Irish border. We present here works from this and other recent exhibitions, amongst them the paintings of Micky Donnelly, the collages and sculpture of Chris Wilson and the photoworks of Willie Doherty, and consider some of the preoccupations that link their diverse styles, the Irish political and economic situation, the cultural and historical relationship with Britain and the English language, the wider relationship with the international artworld and the positive and negative implications of the interest in regionalism that is so much a feature of the 80s. It is an active art scene, which as the variety of styles on show reveals, should perhaps not so much be regarded as an isolated region as a dialogue between the particularities of its situation and the wider concerns and trends of contemporary art. Galleries such as the Orchard Gallery in

Derry, Ferensky's in Belfast and the William Hyde Gallery in Dublin are active not only in showing works by Irish artists but a full range of international exhibitions, and many Irish artists have worked or studied abroad at some point.

Christopher Coppock in his commentary on *A Line of Country; Three Artists from Northern Ireland* at the Cornerhouse in Manchester in 1987 (featuring Anthony Davies, Willie Doherty and Christopher Wilson), considers the possibly negative effects of interest in areas such as Ireland to be part of the Post-Modern phenomenon: '. . . one of the consequences of Post-Modernism was that it caused the culture-capitals in part, to turn their attention from the major centres of art to the art of zones on the periphery; though the intention was not to create genuine dialogue with the cultural, social, political or even historical determinants of those regions but to solve the increasingly redundant marketability of late Modernism. As a result expectations have been heightened in the provinces and an excessive and renewed interest in the vernacular has evolved. The irony of this in the context of Northern Ireland is profound. After years of seeking integration with the "global conversation", artists are now beginning to address the "native" attributes they were so keen to shed. In this light, the concept of a specific Northern Irish visual art is ripe for exploitation. Indeed the recent "Scottish arts experience" provides some artists on this side of the Irish Sea with an alarming example of the way regional identity can be commodified, neatly packaged and made accessible for palates all over the Western world.' Whilst sceptical as to the real value of this interest for the positive development of the plastic arts in Ireland, as opposed to the value for those involved in the commercial art market, he admits that it has led nevertheless to the beneficial development of new opportunities for younger artists.

The selectors of the *Irland-Deutschland Exchange* exhibition noted that in comparison to their West German counterparts, the artists selected were more traditional and less diverse in their materials and that the hierarchy of media culminating with oil painting still appears to dominate. Although many of the works actually chosen were small works on paper, only one artist, Willie Doherty, is a photographer, and only one, Tina O'Connell, currently studying at Chelsea, is a woman. The photoworks of Willie Doherty prove a notable exception. Born in Derry, Northern Ireland, in 1959, Doherty has been closely associated with the Orchard Gallery and has exhibited in the UK and USA as well as Ireland. He works with photography (mainly black and white, although in 1988 he had an exhibition of colour works at the Oliver Dowling Gallery, Dublin) and texts, based on his intimate knowledge of his home environment, he complements his visual imagery with allusive texts, both of which can be read as general statements and not necessarily as specific to their particular Irish situation. Works such as *Fog Icè* combine evocative imagery with vague hints of menace in the ironic use of the texts 'Shrouding' and 'Pervading'. His works also question the images presented in conventional sensationalist news photographs of Derry, presenting a deep inside understanding of the place yet paradoxically 'there's a suggestion that despite the appearance of normality . . . there's something that's unseen and something that isn't normally acknowledged.'

No doubt more women and artists in a variety of media will emerge in the future, as Sean McCrum acknowledges, and maybe the international selection policy of the *Irland-Deutschland Exchange* as a touring showpiece to take to Germany affected the way artists were chosen. One such person not included is installation artist Kathy Prendergast, whose work was in the *Open Futures* exhibition at Birmingham's Ikon Gallery in 1988; a former winner of the Henry Moore Foundation fellowship and RCA travel awards, she has worked in video as well as with sculptural installations. Although now based in London, she was born in Dublin and studied at the National College of Art in Dublin and the Royal College of Art. Another is Eithne Jourdan, whose work was exhibited at London's Paton Gallery in February 1989. Her interest is not in 'Irishness' but femininity, which she explores through large, expressive, primitivistic heads that fill the canvas in broad strokes and sombre colours.

Sean McCrum considers that as a relatively isolated region, on the periphery of Europe, where urbanisation and industrialisation came late, much art between the 50s and 70s was locked into a form of introverted provincialism, but that while international non-representational work became fashionable: 'figuration was never downgraded to the level at which it was in mainland Europe or the USA. It did become defensive, nervously self-protective and so introverted. It needed the infusion, which came from an international re-examination of figuration, starting in the mid-70s, to re-establish its vigour. That return to figuration, similarly to what happened in the Federal Republic of Germany and the rest of Europe and the USA, provided artists with a vehicle for including the examination of their own background in their work.'

Obviously questions of identity and the presence of the Troubles loom large in many of the works – as in the works of Chris Wilson, or the strong charcoal drawings of Andrew Coombes which use the obvious influence of the German Expressionists to explore the Belfast urban scene, but these preoccupations should not be allowed to obscure the individuality of the different artists. The work of Michael Mulcahy is also a response to *other* cultures resulting from his travels in Australia and Polynesia as well as his interest in Irish myths and legends. The work of Micky Donnelly whilst clearly drawing from his Irish heritage should be viewed in the wider context of the British and European revival of interest in symbolism and allegory so prevalent in the 80s, a revival of particular value to someone interested in exploring the Ulster situation. Similarly with Christopher Wilson, although the maps stuck on to works in his *Interior World* series make socio-political references to Belfast and the sectarian divide, his are personal works. Both graphically strong and with layers of meaning, they have an individual and personal symbolism that addresses questions of the artist's situation as much as they do their geographical location, and the use of collage is part of the international art heritage of the 20th century. Slavka Sverakova who selected Wilson for the exhibition *3 Critics 3 Artists* at Fenderesky Art Gallery in 1987 described his work as 'rooted in a heroic Modernist Tradition, in them the idea and material celebrate each other, and the images obtained command a right to belong to this specific society. Both early 20th-century strategies that of collage and that of closed form showed the worry of how to obtain truth and how to present it.' and quotes Christopher Wilson himself describing the interaction between his work and environment: '"the North . . . feeds my imagination . . . I aim to extend (the work) beyond local concerns"'. Wilson is also an impressive sculptor, as seen in his hollow forms in welded steel, such as *When the Shadow Threatened.*

Joan Fowler writing about the work of Micky Donnelly in connection with his 1987 exhibition at the Orchard Gallery, Derry, has written analytically of the symbolic language used in his paintings. The lily is a recurrent image in his compositions, gentle images in soft colours, that reveal the ambiguity of his symbols of Ireland, there is both the white Easter lily that commemorates the 1916 Easter Rising and the orange lily still used to decorate the summer marches of the Orange order: '. . . the symbols used are not so much individualistic as drawn from traditions within Ireland . . . These works pose lily with lily, James Connolly with Lord Carson, the upholder of Unionism. In one sense they pose what is obvious about the conflict between Unionism and Republicanism, but in another sense there is nothing which is obvious because it is rare for these emblems and oracles to be investigated from, as it were, base level. Either these images are assimilated on an almost unconscious level as part of the experience of growing up in Northern Ireland, or they are featured in a purely academic forum in the textbooks of 20th-century Irish history. It seems to be important that for the sake of self-discovery the gap is straddled. For Micky Donnelly these paintings are a way of working through personal experience in order to come to terms with the implications of what they represent, and as such the paintings relate to a good many other Irish people.' Although political, these are not the angry, crusading politics of a Howson or a Currie, but more subtle, perhaps mournful, personal reflections on the complexity of a situation.

———— * ————

FREEZE
Angela Bulloch

Exhibition views showing works by, *Above*: Angela Bulloch, Simon Patterson, Mat Collishaw; *Below L*:
Richard Patterson, Stephen Park, Angus Fairhurst, Anya Gallaccio; *Below R*: Angela Bulloch

In an unusual setting, stuck between warehouses, factories and building sites, the exhibition, *Freeze*, set out to show off young contemporary art. Curated by Damien Hirst, *Freeze* opened on August the 7th in an old building awaiting redevelopment in London's docklands. This exhibition held in three parts showed the work of 16 young artists – the title *Freeze* coming from Matthew Collishaw's piece *Bullet Hole*, where an image of a gun-shot wound is preserved or freeze-framed, in the same way the exhibition is now frozen as a significant event of 1988.

Bullet Hole, which was shown in both the first and final parts of the exhibition, was the most controversial work included. This piece is a close-up photographic image, in colour, of a bullet wound in a human head, enlarged to billboard size and back-lit by 15 separate light boxes. The division of the image into 15 units objectifies it, but does little to subdue the 'matter-of-fact' horror of this detail taken from a medical autopsy book. Hair radiates from the central bloody wound. What do we think of when confronted by such an aberration? The image can be read in several ways: as a fantastic indicator of death 'as seen on TV' in larger than life programmes, or an enticing or offensive display of a sexual hole, it is also an exposure of a fatal wound

showing the unreality of death, as unreal as strawberries in a supermarket advertisement. The contention of this piece lies within the ambiguity of its purpose. Collishaw does not imply any moral position, he simply shows us the cause of death, in full colour on a grand scale.

Essentials is the title of Abigail Lane's two-part floor based sculpture shown in *Freeze* Part I. The white starched cotton cloths are buttoned down the middle and draped over two separate structures. The cloths disguise whatever underlying framework sustains them and the line of buttons provocatively indicates the way to reveal the hidden interior. These sculptures are loosely geometric, one like a cube, the other triangular. They resemble religious gowns or surgical tents which might be used in an operating theatre.

Placed high in the rafters of the building were Damien Hirst's box sculptures. They were made specifically for the first part of the exhibition and were arrangements of multicoloured cardboard boxes coated with gloss paint. His spot paintings, shown in the final part were more interesting examples of his work. 150 circles, also in gloss, were painted directly on to the wall. Each spot was a different colour and painted to form a regular, spaced pattern. This pattern is predetermined but the choice of colour is arbitrary or subjective. The two paintings in the show are the same in every way except for the placing of their edge. In one painting the bottom row ends with half circles and in the other the right-hand end column is cut short. This imaginary line relates to the edge of the wall, where one wall coincides with another or meets the floor. The spots seem to hover in front or recede into the wall in a deceptive way. Angus Fairhurst's work is similar to Hirst's in his choice of two systems, one predicate and the other arbitrary. Fairhurst's boards are marked out into grids of four by one and in each section he has painted a single brushstroke or drilled a hole. The variant which he highlights is the position of the hole within each rectangle, or the impossibility of achieving the same hand-painted stroke. This process could be an endless one but when he has covered two equal sized boards he stops.

Fiona Rae's painting *Skat* has nine separate colourful compositions painted on to a white background, in three rows of three. Within each configuration, tentatively painted brushstrokes support, sustain or lean against more solid but still amorphous areas of colour. These motifs of lines and shapes are balanced, but the drips of paint down the canvas make their equilibrium seem precarious. If these ingenious balancing acts were subject to gravity, as the drips are, they would surely tumble. Gravity is an unsettling force in Rae's painting as it is in Lala Meredith-Vulja's photographs. In one image, a cup and saucer float past a woman's face. With closer examination, we see that the woman is submerged in water. The effect of gravity looks incongruous within the order Meredith-Vulja has created. In another image the woman is shown dressed upside-down, with her skirt covering her head and her feet in the places for her hands. The woman is displaced even within the clothes she wears. This is another example of Meredith-Vulja's peculiar order.

Michael Landy, Gary Hume and Simon Patterson present either a material, the essence of an object or a name. Their work achieves clarity through the reduction of their subjects. Michael Landy, who since *Freeze* has shown at Karsten Schubert in London, Tanja Grunert Gallery in Cologne and at the Grey Art Space in New York, had three large, blue, tarpaulin wall pieces in the first exhibition. These were clipped and draped into their final state with no essential change to the original material. These expansive fields of colour are reminiscent of landscape, but they are more pertinently displays of a simple and functional commodity. Gary Hume showed a series of three paintings which were hung close to the ground and spaced evenly on one wall. Their thick mint-green gloss paint surfaces are disturbed by overpainted round windows and fingerplates. In essence they are tall, closed double doors, like those found in hospitals. The paintings are titled *Mint Green Doors 1-3*. Simon Patterson makes word paintings. These words are names of politicians, astronauts and film stars all from recent times. *Sadat Carter Begin* in American typeface is significant of a moment in history. *Elizabeth Taylor* and *Richard Burton* each printed on separate canvases, presents this couple as two equally powerful personalities.

Over the past five years London galleries have begun to take on younger artists. The Lisson Gallery started first with Julian Opie and more recently with Grenville Davey. Anthony d'Offay Gallery now represents Gerrard Williams. Nicola Jacobs Gallery shows Lisa Milroy and Joanna Kirk. Waddington Gallery have taken on Ian Davenport, a recent art school graduate on the merits of his degree show. He was one of the participating artists in *Freeze* as were Gary Hume and Michael Landy who are now represented by Karsten Schubert. With this new tendency to show younger artists it is no surprise that *Freeze* has caught the attention of the media, in the form of several reviews and a television report on *The Late Show* on BBC2. More than half the participating artists in *Freeze* have been offered future shows, making it possible for this new trend in British art to continue to flourish.

L to R: Abigail Lane, *Essentials*, 1988, starched cotton; Damien Hirst, *Boxes*, 1988, gloss paint on cardboard boxes

PETER RANDALL-PAGE

Wayside Carving, 1988, stone, New Milestones Project, Dorset

SPACES, PLACES AND LANDMARKS
Environmental Art
Rupert Martin

Kier Smith, *The Iron Road*, 1986, Jarrah wood, Forest of Dean Sculpture Project

Rupert Martin discusses the origins of environmental art from Moore's placing of figures in the open air, to Richard Long and David Nash, and looks at the work of young artists, such as Peter Randall-Page and Keir Smith in the Forest of Dean. Working with surprisingly varied materials and subject-matter, they produce artworks that relate to both place and public and are particularly appropriate in the ecologically concerned 80s.

A distinction can be drawn with environmental art between places and spaces, between the changing character of a place with its layers of history, and the more neutral gallery space, which the artist can temporarily make his own. Some artists choose to work in both domains, recognising the different connotations which are imparted to their work. Whilst the work of Richard Long and Andy Goldsworthy is predominantly made outdoors using natural materials, their work can be conveyed into the gallery space through the medium of photography and the written word. The photograph mediates between the uninhabited place and the public space, and it also mediates between the transience of the work and the more permanent imprint made by the light emanating from it. A further dimension is added by the artist bringing material from the land into the gallery space and composing a work within the parameters of that space. Richard Long's *Magpie Line*, shown recently at the Tate Gallery, Liverpool, requires an act of the imagination to complete it, with its suggestion of infinite extension. Wolfgang Laib's rectangles of pure pollen bring to mind the meditative process of gathering the pollen, which glows with an inner radiance coming from the accumulation of these myriad particles of life. A similar reverence for nature as a life-giving force is apparent in the works of Garry Miller, whose photograms reveal the transparency of each fragile leaf, illuminated from within as if by a divine light. The mystical dimension to Laib's and Miller's work is combined with a sensitivity to the fragility of nature and the delicate balance that is required in our relationship to God's creation.

To work in the environment, to evolve a sculpture within a certain place or with a place in mind, to collaborate with the processes of nature requires a certain humility and an understanding of the transience of things. Even the most durable materials such as stone and iron corrode or crack when exposed to the elements. The best works are therefore those which in their choice of materials, scale and position acknowledge that the place is more important than the object and that any intervention is at best semi-permanent. The ethos of the museum to preserve and conserve, cannot apply to works of art in the environment, although it is important that maintenance is carried out for both aesthetic and safety purposes.

The concept of the Sculpture Park lies somewhere in between the museum and the land, aspiring to the freedom of the open-air setting, but confined by the boundaries of the park and the civilising notion of the 'landscape'. They continue the 18th-century concept of art being a tasteful adjunct to nature, a humanising of the land that implies ownership and decorum. In his urge to possess the land, man has to leave his mark upon it, whether by planting a flag, constructing earthwork fortifications, placing an obelisk on the top of a hill or digging a mine-shaft into it. By contrast the most enduring works of art are those which like the Aboriginal Songlines live in the imagination and belong to the whole culture. In their belief the land itself is continually being sung into existence through the activity of the imagination, and landmarks have an interior significance, a hidden value. As Bruce Chatwyn wrote in *The Songlines*: 'In theory, at least, the whole of Australia could be read as a musical score. There was hardly a rock or creek in the country that could not or had not been sung.' The nearest we have come to this kind of freedom is in the work of Richard Long, a latter-day nomad whose subtle and often transitory marks on the land are kept alive in the photographic image or in words which evoke place and passage. Richard Long's vocabulary of forms – circle, line, spiral – are common to many cultures, and relate to earlier ways of making marks on the land. Environmental artists often make connections with the religious origins of stone circles and standing stones in their choice of forms and materials. In an increasingly secular age, this is both more difficult and more important as an alternative to the urban-based consumer culture which dominates our media. By putting us in touch with nature, works of art can help us to identify with places and alert us to the 'unseen landscapes' about which Paul Nash wrote, 'unseen because not seen'. The Romantic notion of the spirit of place is seen afresh in the light of a rigorous logic, a clarity of expression characteristic of the Classical idiom with its emphasis on proportion.

Perhaps the best known examples of sculpture in the open air, the form that most environmental art in this country takes, are the works of Henry Moore purchased in the 1950s by Sir William Keswick and sited with great sensitivity on the edge of a remote

and putting them in the landscape. The new approach has involved artists getting to know a stretch of land and evolving ideas for sculpture out of their response to a specific place. This process has been developed most notably in Grizedale Forest where with the collaboration of the Forestry Commission, annual residencies have been taking place since 1978, when David Nash became the first artist to work there. This approach exemplified in the work of Nash is a new form of the truth to materials philosophy of the 1930s, and is also partly a reaction to the Pop artists' love of plastic, fibre-glass and other artificial materials. All except one of the sculptures in Grizedale are made using indigenous wood and stone. Nash's contributions included channelling the element of water through fallen branches in *Wooden Waterway*, and revealing the inner vitality of the tree in the sculpture *Running Table*. Nash's attitude to the elements and to nature underlies the ethos of the Grizedale Project which has had a significant influence on the development of outdoor sculpture in this country.

The same truth to materials and propriety of placing is apparent in the *New Milestones Project* inaugurated by Common Ground with a pilot scheme in Dorset. Their method differs in

Forest of Dean, *L to R*: Stuart Frost, *Bracken Ring*, 1986; Yvette Martin, *The Four Seasons*, 1986; Cornelia Parker, *Hanging Fire*, 1988, cast iron

moor in Dumfriesshire. The photographs of these works have been often reproduced and have been influential in the development of the idea of placing works of art in the landscape. Moore's own comments show how much he was aware of the way in which a landscape can bring out one aspect of a sculpture. Writing of his *Standing Figure*, the first sculpture to be sited at Glenkiln he said: 'In the bleak and lonely setting of a grouse moor, the figure itself becomes an image of loneliness, and on its outcrop of rock, its lean, skeletonic form stands out sharp and clear against the sky, looking as if stripped to the bone by the winds of several centuries.' In a similar way the *Upright Motif No 1* becomes a part of the landscape, appearing from the distance like an ancient Celtic cross. The siting of this sculpture took into account both the lie of the land and the local usage, since it occupies the place where the artist on his visit to Glenkiln saw a shepherd surveying his sheep. The identification of the sculpture with the place is complete in the name by which it is now known, the *Glenkiln Cross*.

However well the sculptures by Moore have been placed, giving them enough space in which to breathe, there has recently been a movement away from this idea of collecting works of art

that they aim to involve local people in the process of commissioning a work of art that in some way celebrates the land they inhabit. Two of these commissions were organised in collaboration with the Weld Estate which adjoins a stretch of unspoilt coastline at East Lulworth. The response of both artists was similar in that both sought, in the words of Peter Randall-Page, 'to make a work which would relate to the intimacy of human scale – something on which to refocus the senses before returning to the enormity of land, sea and sky.' Both he and Simon Thomas chose a theme and material that was appropriate to the place. For Peter Randall-Page, the abundance of fossils in the area and the rhythms of the hills, 'sweeping in broad rounded curves', provided the starting point for three shell-like forms. The material is a local limestone, blue Purbeck marble, consisting of tiny fossilised gastropod shells, and is commonly found in church architecture. The sense of preciousness, created by the material which is now no longer quarried, is further enhanced by the placing of each subject in a dry-stone wall niche to suggest a wayside shrine before which one can pause for contemplation and recollection. An indicator of how people have responded is evident in the way that the rounded surfaces have been polished by constant touching, in the same way that the knee of Moore's *Madonna and Child* in St Matthew's Church, Northampton has been made smooth by people touching the sculpture. The freedom which people have to explore the tactile dimension of sculpture, denied them in museums or exhibitions, is one of the strongest attractions of outdoor sculpture.

Simon Thomas' four carvings of enlarged seed forms relate to the usage of this particular stretch of land for the cultivation of wheat, one of the earliest such sites in the country. The sculptures thus draw attention to the history and unique character of the place, and are made out of weathered oak from the estate. Their placing in a field where sheep graze is also fortuitous. As Joanna Morland who set up the pilot scheme in Dorset writes in the book, *New Milestones: Sculpture, Community and the Land,* 'the oak wooden seeds appear to be much used and enjoyed by the sheep as scratching posts and wind breaks, and the oak has benefitted from the quantities of lanolin from the sheep's fleeces which burnishes and protects the wood. A happy co-existence!'

Both these works of art involve sequences or clusters of small objects which enlarge the scope of the sculpture, and actively involve people in walking alongside, round or through the herd through the forest are caught in silhouette, with their secret 'thoughts' revealed in brightly coloured emblematic flower, tree, fish and bird forms on their head, back or tail. Whilst the subject of both these works is appropriate to the Forest of Dean, their materials are not; Keir Smith's railway sleepers were made for use in the London Underground from Jarrah Eucalyptus, an oily wood which delays rotting, and Zadok Ben David's deer are prosaically made by applying a black stained car-filler to a metal armature. Although such materials are not indigenous, they are right for the wet weather conditions which are common in the Dean.

By contrast the wood used in the work of Magdalena Jetelovà and Bruce Allan are appropriate but their subjects, a giant chair-like structure entitled *Place*, and a staircase that leads nowhere entitled *Observatory*, seem to be out of place. And yet, displaced in location and in scale, their very incongruity and simplicity of form is effective. As with the stained glass *Cathedral* window it is the area they occupy and the space that they include which is of vital importance. Kevin Atherton's concept includes the tall pillared trees which you walk through to reach the east window of the Cathedral. The sculpture acts as a catalyst, drawing

L to R: Kevin Atherton, *Cathedral*, 1986, stained glass, Forest of Dean; Simon Thomas, *Seed Forms*, 1988, oak, New Milestones Project Dorset

interconnected elements. This aspect of participation through walking is a vital part of works of art in the open, since it enables them to be seen from near and far, from different viewpoints, with different horizons, and in varying weather conditions which affect the mood of the sculpture. In the *Forest of Dean Sculpture Project* several artists have made similar clusters to explore, which relate also to the character of the Dean. Keir Smith's *The Iron Road*, consists of 20 railway sleepers embedded in a curve of the old railway line from Cinderford to Lydney. Out of each sleeper an image has been carved that relates to some aspect of the forest whether rural or industrial. Each sleeper can be looked at in isolation, or read as a sequence of images which compose a poem. The sculptures do not make up a narrative but through recurring images compose a kind of elegy to the intrinsic life of the forest which man has helped to shape. They add to the landmarks which have been left from centuries of mining, smelting and forestry, the aim being to reinterpret the forest through the eye of the imagination. Another sequence is the group of seven deer by Israeli artist, Zadok Ben David, which comments on the dividing line between fact and fantasy, reality and the imagination. The black shapes of the deer moving in a attention not just to itself but to the wood in which it is placed, and to the connection between the sanctuary of the forest and the gloom of the Cathedral with its forest of pillars. Placed on the brow of a hill overlooking the Cannop Valley, the animated figure of Magdalena Jetelovà's sculpture surveys the landscape. It is a place, a kind of woodhenge which we can enter, whose portals frame the landscape and direct our gaze outwards to include the length of the wooded Cannop Valley. The experience reminds one of Moore's eloquent description of the *Recumbent Figure*, 1936, made for Chermayeff's house overlooking the Sussex Downs, in which he speaks of becoming aware of 'giving outdoor sculpture a far-seeing gaze. My figure looked out across a great sweep of the Downs, and her gaze gathered in the horizon.'

As *Place* draws our gaze outwards to embrace the horizon, so Cornelia Parker's work, *Hanging Fire* draws the eye upward into the crown of a clump of five sycamore trees from which it is suspended 15 feet above the ground. The canopy of the trees creates a dark green space in which the bright orange of the rusting cast-iron glows like fire. Through the work Cornelia Parker explores the symbolism of crowns and fire, and uses an indigenous metal, iron, cast in the nearby Cannop Foundry: 'Fire has many spiritual associations, in a biblical sense as the manifestation of the Holy Ghost, or in the metaphoric sense describing, for example, the vigour of thought, the warmth of affection or burning passion', while 'A falling crown points to the subconscious, the roots beneath the tree and the source of regeneration.' The colour of the rusted crown of flames enables it both to blend with the leaves in autumn and to be distinct from them in the summer.

In recent years there has been an increase in environmental art projects, outdoor exhibitions, garden festivals and public art commissions. A new way of working has emerged which does not depend on the commercial galleries who are often unable to take on the younger artists. Making work in and for the environment offers young artists the opportunity to prove themselves, and to develop their skill and their vision in difficult terrain and in sometimes daunting weather conditions. At the same time the problems to be found in making work outdoors are not to be underestimated either by the artist or the commissioning agency.

Environmental art functions on a number of levels, generating a new and healthy interest in art on the part of people who may never visit an art gallery, exposing sculpture to the vagaries of the weather, helping to inculcate a respect for the environment and an increased awareness of an ecology that holds man, animal and plant in a fragile equilibrium, fostering a renewed concern for spiritual values which go against the grain of our rational, materialistic society, and generating new works of art by a younger generation of artists, inspired by the work of Henry Moore, Ian Hamilton Finlay, Richard Long, David Nash and Andy Goldsworthy to work in harmony with nature and expose their work in the light of day. If the 1980s is the decade which saw the revival of painting, and the 1990s promises to become the decade in which sculpture comes to the fore, then the greatest scope for the development of sculptural ideas could lie in its interaction with and integration into the environment which we are once more beginning to cherish.

Simon Thomas, *Burning Bush*, 1986, beechwood, Camley Street Natural Park

Chris Drury, *Above L to R: Shelter for the 4 Days on Muckish, Co Donegal; Falling Water Stupa; Below: Stone Lavo – Mageroya Island, Finland*

KATE WHITEFORD AND CHRIS DRURY

Art, too, has its share of creation myths. One of them features the rival painters Zeuxis and Parrhasios. In a bravura display of skill, Zeuxis paints a picture which includes the depiction of a bunch of grapes which some birds take for the real thing, flying down to settle and peck at the pigment. But it is Parrhasios who wins the day for he paints on a wall a veil, a veil so lifelike (yes, lifelike) that Zeuxis turns towards him and asks Parrhasios to lift the veil and show what he has painted behind it.

The French psychoanalyst Jacques Lacan deployed this tale in a seminar, of 4th March 1964, that had as its topic the eye, the gaze and picturing.[1] The grapes lured the birds, they proved a decoy, not because of any excess of verisimilitude, perhaps, but because they served well enough to do that job; that is, those dabs and daubs of paint played the sign strictly enough for the birds. However, the veil presented itself to the gaze as an appearance that claims it is that which gives the appearance, and consequently incites our desire for that which lies behind it. Whether that is taken as the Real, or the Idea, or some authentically apprehensible Being, it is what is intimated as beyond the representation that gives to the veil the power of the icon. Indeed, when it is a veil that faces us, then even though it hides nothing, even though there is nothing behind these words, no anterior motive to this image, nonetheless that absence or loss becomes invested with potency. The veil teases our bridled desire to see.

Even the most cursory glance around us and at the fatefulness of images and representations in history confirms a belief that it is only the powerful icons that are broken, only the potent images which are suppressed. Why else is force mobilised against them, unless they themselves have power? It is not prudence, or guilt, alone that produces the suspicion that whispered secrets are true, and that they are about us. (They are.) A current strategy in Kate Whiteford's work is to make the construction of the veil so conspicuous that we attend not to it but to our collusion in its construction. I gaze hard at the picture, led on by the allure of the veil, only to discover that the veil is a lure.

In a recently completed and prize-winning series of drawings, *Logos*, simple graphic outlines (a fish, a moon, comb, arch, snake) are just discernible as the faint markers left by the application of charcoal, densely, to the remainder of the surface. It is as though the charcoal marks have pushed the image back and back, giving the surface a velvety depth which has been built up over time. Each drawing seems to display a tenderness, to have become invested with a careful concentration we have lost: these ghosts not only haunt the once-upon-a-time and the not-yet, they also are the almost-images of what

might-have-been. What is there to be seen (as the image is nudged into sight by the coherent avoidances of the artist's hand) is something which is easy to *grasp*; an image rustling in the wings of visibility persisting, potent, amidst the failure to obliterate or wear down or out. The prize that my gaze takes is not that image itself – which is so often banal and unexciting, *once named* – but the foregrounded awareness of the history of my looking as I probe for the thing which has yet to be fully disclosed. Fumbling in the dark has its own pleasures, discovers its own worlds, whether or not I find what I was looking for. If the sense of 'something's missing' is active in these drawings, then its aspect of reclaiming the presence of the past in the present – and thus of rehabilitating the present itself – is even more apparent in a recent series of large paintings. Once again, the images snare the viewer into confronting the idea that is enacted when somebody's looking. Their greater abstraction draws attention without diversion to the crackling optical flicker they produce to the eye. Traversing the passage of time, the eye may accommodate itself to the visual stimulus. But as the retinal fizz subsides, so a new confusion appears: the paired colours of the canvas relate as image and after-image, and staring at the picture invokes the uncanny sensation of being unsure whether what one sees is the image of the visual stimulus or the image of the absence of that image. By placing the seeing eye in circuit with the canvas, the dependence of the truth-telling character of vision upon the unfolding relationships of perception is vividly dramatised. When I see true is it with my eyes open or shut? Time itself acquires a thickness. We can tug at the present, and find it rooted in time; the absence that lurks behind the veil of Kate Whiteford's work is a measure of the loss we sustain when we consider the present as effected by a rupture with the past rather than as developing from it.

In the end, then, her work is not nostalgic, in the sense of looking backward in a vain and futile desire for regression, but rather it recaptures the present as a place of possibilities (not all of which may be realised) and hope (which may be disappointed). To experience the present in this way is one aspect of what it is to be at home in the world as it is. Despite the general 20th-century lament that in our urban, industrial, always mediated existence, we are decoupled from our social and natural environment (and so disconnected from ourselves), rootless, homeless, nonetheless we are still capable of experiencing moments of completeness and reconciliation. Such moments, and the objects and memories which are their residue and token, tend to be touched with a special brightness. The chubby green fountain pen, 30 years old now, with which I write these notes may not

be one of those that the manufacturer or retailer would like to be remembered by, but it fits my hand to my way of thinking well enough. A childhood memory: lying on my back on a wooden bench in a dark wooden hut, happy with the flickering beaded light that caulks the cracks between the planks, and the sound of water outside. Good to handle, good to remember, good to think: I would say that Kate Whiteford and Chris Drury make images and objects which affirm both the necessity and the realisability of a way of life which is all of these.

It was the custom among the Olglala Sioux, when coming again to the place where a child was born, to place the child on the ground and roll it north, east, south and west. The place where we were born is special to all of us, in much the same way as our name is: it doesn't feel to me like I'm simply *called* 'David', rather I *am* David, that is who I am, and similarly to realise the significance of a place it is not enough to be contingently there (one might as well be elsewhere), one must find a way of recognising the *fittingness* of being there.

Chris Drury's art is steeped in an openness to the particularities of place. He goes into the landscape, often camping, sometimes walking between a starting point and a finishing point which already have spiritual significance to him. He watches and listens to the events around him, and attends as closely on and to the thoughts and dreams that are prompted within him: Drury knows that it pays to take dreams seriously, as do all who set aside their cloak of pretences to mastery, and own to their uncertainty and vulnerability. The places where he walks and camps, and the art work made in keeping with those places, map out a personal 'medicine wheel', emblematic of a topography of meaningful situation.

Drury's best known work is undoubtedly *Medicine Wheel*, 1982-3, a segmented circular frame on which are displayed objects collected day by day throughout one year, surrounding a 12-segmented disc of papers made from pulps of the month's vegetation, and at the centre a mushroom print. Lately, his work has acquired a refined focus and great power in developing objects which relate to themes of enclosure and transformation. These are 'baskets' and 'shelters', whose making requires a detailed knowledge of the materials of an environment and how to use them in the making.[2] The design of the basket provides a poetic container or resting place for Drury's developing understanding of the relationships between his 'inner life' and the environment – in a sense, the basket is a precipitate at the meeting point of the world inside and the world outside. (It is because it is formed at an interface of different but, through it, commensurable discourses that the basket can be read as a species of *diagram.*)

The shelters are made outside, and undergo a metamorphosis before finding their place inside, in a gallery perhaps. The 'shelters' are not so named because Drury hides from the weather in them, rather they are objects which express a sheltering, a dwelling, a preserving in that place, so far as he can realise it. In much the same way, an artist might make a doll-fetish which carries some function of personality without being a person: the difference is, that the material of the doll is of interest only insofar as it can be turned to expressive need, whereas the materials of Drury's shelters, whilst clearly capable of forming the shelter, nonetheless have significance primarily in virtue of their existence independent of his will. Drury's relationship to the stoneness of a stone is fundamental to what a stone shelter expresses. A shelter made 'in the presence of deer' is transformed by weaving a cone from the shelter's thatch and placing it inside the gaunt framework of the shelter: this is what we find indoors. The thatch cone and the skeletal frame fit together aesthetically, not practically, and in that visible remainder, that gap that sheaths the cone, there is a resonant absence, as though the landscape kept its distance.

The baskets and shelter are objects whose simple and poetic determinations consistently provide convincing form. They seem to emerge from conviction, patience and trust in ideas and material, and they have about them a proper awkwardness – prickly, scratchy, untidy and useless. All that they are good for is to hold what we put there – feelings, dreams, and a sense regained of the inevitable possibilities that abound in the world. In this work, the aspiration, and the significance of the aspiration for us, is that the work should be *brought about* by the living, and is the expression of a form of life. Jacques Lacan could have been anticipating Chris Drury's art when, one week later, he said: 'If a bird were to paint would it not be by letting fall its feathers, a snake by casting off its scales, a tree by letting fall its leaves?'

David Reason

Notes

1   The references to the seminars of Jacques Lacan are to the text known as *The Four Fundamental Concepts of Psycho-analysis*, ed Jacques-Alain Miller, trans by Alan Sheridan, Penguin Books, Harmondsworth, 1979.
2   Some of the ideas developed in this article found first expression in: 'The World's Room: Shelters and Baskets: Gathering Place' in *Chris Drury: Shelters and Baskets*, Orchard Gallery Derry 1989 and 'Drawing Lines' in *4 Internationale Triennale Der Zeichnung*, Kunsthalle Nurnburg 1988.

Kate Whiteford, *Sculpture for Calton Hill, Edinburgh*, 1987, Skye marble chippings inset into turf

SHIRAZEH HOUSHIARY

Temple of Dawn, 1987, mud and straw, Munster Sculpture Project

GENERATION GAMES IN SCULPTURE
Tim Marlow

Anish Kapoor, *To Reflect an Intimate Part of the Red*, 1981, pigment and mixed media

Tim Marlow looks at the artworld background that has raised a particular group of sculptors – Cragg, Deacon, Houshiary, Kapoor *et al* – to eminence and designated them as the 'New British Sculpture' and asks whether despite their diversity there is indeed validity in seeing them as a group, that shares formal approaches and concern with the natural world, language and poetry, and as part of a continuing British sculptural tradition.

This year, 1989, marks the last opportunity to include two of the most eminent contemporary British sculptors in a survey of British artists under the age of 40. Born in 1949, both Tony Cragg and Richard Deacon approach the daunting barrier of artistic middle age, the same barrier, incidentally, that Bill Woodrow, Richard Wentworth and Alison Wilding went through last year. At last year's Venice Biennale, Tony Cragg was to have been awarded one of the prizes for artists under the age of 40 but ultimately this was denied him on the grounds that he was already too eminent. One might be tempted to mumble ironically about a rather British sense of fair play in operation. No matter for concern, however, Cragg together with Deacon and others have received wide acclaim on national and international levels. Monthly, even weekly, the art press surveys work by these sculptors, invariably grouping them together. This article seeks to extend analysis of the state of the art of British sculpture to incorporate a look at the state of the artworld which has sought to project them within the restricting confines of a national tradition.

Postwar sculpture in Britain is conceived strongly in terms of a succession of generations passing on the 'torch' of a recently established British sculptural tradition, categorised with a distinct lack of poetic sensibility. The 'New British Sculpture' is but the most recent in a long line of undistinguished (and sometimes undistinguishable) neoterisms which, whilst obviously reflecting relevant critical discourse, have tended to arise from certain collective exhibitions. Two exhibitions in London early in 1965 can be assumed to have played a pivotal role in this respect: *British Sculpture in the Sixties* at the Tate Gallery and *The New Generation* at the Whitechapel. Running concurrently, but essentially in opposition, the former was retrospective whilst the latter was avant-garde in intent. On the admission of its organisers, the Contemporary Art Society exhibited work at the Tate by many sculptors, the spirit of whose work was truly contemporary some ten years before – Butler, Armitage, Chadwick and Meadows, as well as Moore and Hepworth. At the Whitechapel, however, Bryan Robertson initiated the public debut of a group of young sculptors centred around St Martin's School of Art, strongly influenced by the abstract sculpture of Anthony Caro. The nucleus of this group consisted of Philip King, Bill Tucker, Tim Scott, David Annesley and Mike Bolus. These exhibitions, together with the ensuing critical response, established what might tritely but not untruthfully be called the 'generation game': Moore and Hepworth became recognised as the core of an 'older generation'; Butler, Armitage, Chadwick and Meadows were seen as leading figures in the 'middle generation' and the Whitechapel group, more obviously, continued as the 'new generation'.

The concept of 'the new' has a perennial appeal to art historians but in recent decades this has become a British obsession. It has proved difficult to devise a bland collectivism for the generation of artists who followed on from the 'New Generation', not least because in the period loosely described as witnessing 'the de-materialisation of the art object' (Lucy Lippard) towards the end of the 60s, so many attempts were made to label a vast internationally based phenomenon – Conceptual Art, *Arte Povera*, Environmental Art, Micro-Emotive Art, call it what you will – which defies coherent distillation into any one meaningful term. Nevertheless, an attempt was made to survey the work of various British artists working in this expansive field, many of whom had succeeded the 'New Generation' at St Martin's. The occasion was another exhibition, this time at the Hayward Gallery, entitled *The New Art*.

This is the distant etymological background for the bland soubriquet the 'New British Sculpture' favoured today to describe the Cragg, Deacon, Woodrow 'generation'. Superficially, it might be deemed as arid a line of enquiry as taking sculpture beyond objecthood, an activity described by one cynical critic as 'mere navel contemplation'. However analysis shows that it is an integral, if irritating, symptom of the 'generation game' so central to the establishment of a postwar British sculptural 'tradition'. Critical use of the term the 'New British Sculpture' was retrospective beginning around 1984 after the public launching of the latest generation a couple of years or so earlier. In 1981 in what is now perceived to be a seminal show entitled *Objects and Sculpture*, Deacon, Gormley, Kapoor, Woodrow (together with Frenchman Jean-Luc Vilmouth, Edward Allington, Margaret Organ and Peter Randall-Page) were exhibited together for the first time. With the addition of Cragg the nucleus was virtually established. Significantly, the two women in the group, Alison Wilding and Shirazeh Houshiary, were projected into the public arena slightly later, at Kettle's Yard, Cambridge, in 1982. Not since Hepworth and Frink had women been assimilated into the mainstream British tradition whose macho ethos can be traced back to and beyond St Martin's in the 60s.

'Official' sanctioning of the group followed rapidly when, in 1983, the British Council sent work by Cragg, Deacon, Gormley, Kapoor, Wilding and Woodrow to the Biennale Sao Paulo and then to Rio de Janeiro in 1968, three years after the public debut of the post-Caro 'New Generation', the British Council was still devising for international consumption, exhibitions by the previous two generations of British sculptors; recent years have witnessed a swifter response from the art establishment to the art of the present. The catalogue to the 1983 British Council exhibition proudly proclaimed: 'with notable exceptions it is British sculpture rather than British painting which has commanded international attention since 1945'. Obviously, the aim of the exhibition *New Sculpture* was to continue the cultivation of international attention but even though the catalogue was at pains to stress that 'the sculptors in this exhibition constitute neither a group nor precisely a generation' the means to achieve this end centres implicitly around a notion of group identity rooted in the British tradition, borne out explicitly three years later when all seven sculptors were posited as the youngest generation in an exhibition entitled *Entre El Objeto y La Imaginacion: escultura britanica contemporanea* in Madrid, organised jointly by the Spanish Ministerio de Cultura and the British Council. The 15 artists spanned from Paolozzi via Caro and Tucker and then Flanagan, Long and Michael Craig-Martin through to the latest group of seven. In his introduction Julian Andrews expressed the hope that 'the exhibition will bring the weight of old associations to the new work and provide the opportunity to look at the older work with fresh perceptions generated by the new.'

In an information-based culture, with the rapid growth in mass media and art journals since the 60s, one might suppose there are many varied platforms for dissenting voices. Quite so, but our general perceptions about the art of recent decades is conditioned far more by the way that art is exhibited than by any critical discourse. It could be argued, as indeed it often is, that the Modernist paradigm lies at the root of all linear progressivist evils, particularly the formalist polemic which beset British sculpture in the 60s. However, the over-simplified extensions of

this idea – the 'generation game' in other words – is too convenient for exhibition organisers, particularly those that seek to propagate a cultural nationalism. There is little evidence for any Post-Modern ideology influencing the way that museums seek to organise art of the present and recent past.

* * *

In examining more specifically the so-called 'New British Sculpture' in the context of a climate of artistic diversity, one must ask if the British sculptural tradition, established and promoted through a critical and curatorial generation game, is strong enough to withstand a continuation of that same fallacious game. The best British sculpture currently being produced does indeed have various shared concerns. Assimilating many of the diverse lessons of international art from the end of the 60s onwards but returning to a physical, material presence, work is produced which is embodied with content as opposed to purely formalist values. Associational and often metaphorical concerns are cultivated and expressed in work which simultaneously elicits the idea of objecthood and sculpture. As the *Objects and Sculpture* catalogue commented:'(it)seem(s) to refer both to *objects* in the world, and to *sculpture* given some status as a category of special objects separated from the world.'

Ideas, material and objects/images interrelate in the work of current British sculptors but the diversity which this generates is great enough to preclude much meaningful generalisation. The concerns of past 'generations' are drawn upon but in a manner which is unsystematic and unselfconscious. It seems, to use the words of Lewis Biggs, that there is 'a wish to be free of history in the sense of a linear or determined development: and correspondingly they feel free to take from history whatever they wish.'

Landscape, that supposedly quintessential English concern, and the natural world in general are alluded to in various guises – as idea, material, process or image. Cragg has referred to it most overtly. In pieces like *Two Tables and Four Stones* from 1983 intended for the gallery and *Earth Product* from 1987 produced for outside the gallery, he posits the precarious relationship between the natural and designed worlds; landscape and the industrialised world. *Earth Product* depicts a collection of chemical containers scattered over and around three large stones, emptying their lethal contents on to a defenceless landscape. The piece warns of environmental dangers but is neither didactic nor proselytising. It challenges a tendency to glorify the 'found object' and yet, at the same time, evokes a disquieting sense of beauty in man-made and natural objects combined.

Shirazeh Houshiary has used the soil of the earth in many of her works from *Listen to the Tale of the Reed* in 1982 to *The Temple of Dawn* in 1987. In the latter, a combination of mud-clay and straw surrounds a wickerwork structure creating a spiritual vessel or temple on a hill in Münster (for the Münster Sculpture Project in fact). It is made of the earth and resides on the earth. Born in Iran, Houshiary brings an oriental mysticism into play in her sculpture wherein reference to Persian and Sufi legends abound. Likewise, Anish Kapoor – born in India – shares an interest in the metaphysical which manifests itself strongly in his work but bears little relationship to the natural world in the way that Houshiary's work does: 'I wish to make sculpture about belief, or about passion, about experience, that is, outside of material concerns.'

Mention of Kapoor serves to suggest an obtuse example of what Lewis Biggs described as the freedom to take from history whatever is desired. In spite of Kapoor's vehement denials of formalist influence ('I have no formal concerns, I don't wish to make sculpture about form') he has unselfconsciously taken up one of the problems of the post-Caro abstractionists (and indeed of Caro himself), namely the relationship between form and colour. Recently Caro said that 'colour is something which no sculptor has grasped: it's not our language', adding that all too often colour in sculpture is 'used like colour in furniture or painted walls'. In using coloured chalk-powder sprinkled over and around his sensual forms Kapoor frees colour from the restraints of form, giving it an autonomy whilst at the same time suggesting a positive interaction between colour and object. His sculptures arrest the eye with a rare and physical immediacy yet preclude the overwhelming desire to touch them. In this way, he transcends the concerns of formalism and indeed transcends the material world as a whole. The metaphysical effect is supremely individual.

Allusions to other artforms and to poetry in particular are evident in the work of Deacon, Kapoor and Houshiary, but once again the character is heteromorphic. The poetry of Baudelaire (as well as Persian and Sufi myth) has inspired Houshiary in works like *L'Invitation au Voyage* as it has the work of Kapoor, though less obviously so, in works like *A Flower, A Drama like Death*. Back in 1978, Richard Deacon developed a deep interest in Rilke's *Sonnets to Orpheus* and consequently his sculpture began to assume its characteristic lyrical quality. As Richard Cork has mentioned, Deacon's *Falling on Deaf Ears (Nos 1 and 2)* abound with Orphean reference, not least in their subtle evocation of music as well as poetry. Drawing on all the senses bar taste, other sculptures like *Blind, Deaf and Dumb* convey an ironic sense of synaesthesia both in title and, less ironically, in their form and effect. Styling himself more as 'fabricator' than sculptor, Deacon also equates the process of creating objects with language: 'making has some profound relationship to language. One of the prime functions of language is to describe or reform the world. It is something that is neither yours nor mine, but is ours and lies between us and the stuff out there. Making is not dissimilar.'

Even in this brief survey, it becomes clear that there is a cultural diversity prevalent in the 'New British Sculpture' which defies the blandness of that collective term. In turn this artistic interplay has led to an increased critical interplay. In this journal, for instance, in the last two years, wider artistic themes from Classical and Romantic strands to a popular or Pop Art based lineage have been superimposed on the sculpture of the last three decades. Whilst inevitably still rooted in a paradigmatic art historical perspective, they offer some hope at least of breaking down some of the fallacies of an oversimplified 'generation game'. Even this faint hope however must be tempered by the current facts of life or, rather, facts of life in the London art world: the unparalleled importance of British art schools in the development of a nation's artists, particularly those in London. No other country reflects this phenomenon so strongly. No other country finds life so focused into one city either. Although the pre-eminence of St Martin's, in terms of British sculpture, has diminished, strands of continuity can still be traced. Both Deacon and Woodrow studied there. Likewise, Cragg, Deacon, Wentworth and Wilding all studied at the Royal College at various times. More significantly, Gormley, Julian Opie and Grenville Davey all studied at Goldsmiths' College of Art in successive generations of students (and Deacon, among others, has taught there on a part-time basis). Goldsmiths' in the 80s offers only the faintest of parallels with St Martin's in the 60s but it is ripe for critical analysis and, more worrying, offers a possible focal point for would-be perpetrators of the 'generation game'. Opie and Grenville Davey are the youngest sculptors represented by the Lisson Gallery which also represents Cragg, Deacon, Woodrow, Wentworth, Kapoor and Houshiary. Collectively, they are sometimes referred to as the 'Lisson School' (a term rejected, it must be added, by the gallery's director Nicholas Logsdail). One waits with trepidation for the announcement that a 'New Lisson School' has emerged, and correspondingly, a new 'New British Sculpture' (or perhaps even a more international prefix, the dreaded 'Neo-') being brought into play.

Tony Cragg, *On the Savannah*, 1988, metal

ANTONY GORMLEY

Above: *12 Hours. The Beginning, The Middle, The End*, 1986-7, lead, fibreglass, plaster, air. 'I think my ambition is to make things that are visible in the light about where we come from – which is darkness. To make things that stand outside time which can be experienced in time, and that either come from the point where time ended or the point before time began. It's an attempt to make an object that is a concentration, a physical equivalent for a span of time. It could be a day, an hour, a lifetime, an era. I think we experience partially, sequentially, but eternity is one thing. Sculpture pertains to the single object: to wholeness. This piece is an attempt to reconcile partiality with wholeness.' *Below*: *Landing II*, 1987-8, lead, fibreglass, plaster, air. 'They are both moulds of me. All of the work is an attempt to make me the other and to give it a strangeness or to deposit my own position in a thing out there. My own feeling is that it's about the fear of space as much as it might be about sex or a coming together. But I think it's the effect of space on those two bodies that causes the attraction which then becomes a sexual analogy. I'm trying to associate planetary bodies and the way they behave gravitationally with sexual bodies. I'm interested in the way that reproduction in cells isn't about two separate things coming together to produce a third, but one thing that divides into two. The line that divides and joins those two figures becomes very important and the way the arms work across it . . . With these works I've been taking far greater liberties but I think it's very easy to get self indulgent. I'm very aware that it's easy to make sculpture but quite difficult to communicate. It's easy to make things that articulate space, but for me the challenge is how you introduce something else that has a different function, a different intensity. My concern has been not to allow the art to get in the way of a healing function. In a way we've been dealing with beauty for a long time, what we've got to get down to is something more vital: survival.'

EDWARD ALLINGTON

Above: *An Apollo Admiring Two Vases*, 1988, black painted wood, resin and plastic; *Below L to R*: *Saturnus*, 1988; *Three, Four and Five*, 1988, both ink and emulsion on paper on canvas. The drawings and monochrome sculptures of Edward Allington translate the myths of Classical antiquity into claustrophobic modern settings where collections of dislocated, often repetitive fragments of architecture, sculpture and other artefacts have become categorically confused, questioning the authenticity of language codes through the artificial, playful nature of their presentation; above all creating a sense of loss of continuity with the past. 'For me with Classical reference there is no nostalgia, it is no more than a mode, a basis for thinking, a starting point.'

NICOLA HICKS

Above: *La Confidente*, 1987, bronze cast; *Below L to R*: *I Can Do That II (cow, cat, bird)*, 1988; *Over & Over Again (cow)*, 1988, wire, straw and painted plaster. Nicola Hicks creates aggressively unsentimental, life-size sculptures of greyhounds, hogs and other 'beasts', moulded from a rough texture of clay, straw and painted plaster, occasionally cast in bronze. Her 'savage' and even 'violent' sculptures contain a sense of raw energy and a primitive, emotive force that relates to the artist's creative process, evolving to some extent from large charcoal drawings on brown paper, many drawn from life and revealing her studies of anatomy.

VERONICA RYAN

Above L to R: Concealed, 1988, plaster, lead, *In Memory*, 1988, plaster, dried flowers; *Below: Trough*, 1988, bronze, dried flowers.
'I'm very interested in the relationship between verbal and visual language . . . metaphor gives me the possibility to describe experience visually. . . I am concerned with identity, place, history and how they determine the way one is positioned in a culture.'
Ryan aims 'to explore boundaries' and spatial concepts and to make her ideas accessible by combining lead, plaster and bronze with 'non-sculpture' materials such as dried flowers, to express her interest in the nature of organic forms.

Above L to R: Powell, *Cowhorn Platform*; *Martial Music*; *Below L to R*: Ellis, *Ghosts*, 1988; Geliot, *Music with Menaces – Creeping Horn*, 1988

NEW ART IN WALES
David Briers

Life Support System, performance photograph

Whilst lacking the coherent identity and high profile of the young Scottish artists, opportunities for young artists in Wales have recently increased with grants, exhibition spaces and public commissions. Sculpture is probably the strongest field, using unorthodox materials influenced by *Arte Povera* and environmental art, but David Briers also notes the presence of many young painters and of performances where art and theatre cross boundaries.

The closing pages of Eric Rowan's book *Art in Wales: An Illustrated History 1850-1980*, commissioned by the Welsh Arts Council and published in 1985, include the following observation: '. . . there now exist in Wales more artists than at any time in the past, more studios in which they can work, more galleries to exhibit their work, more patrons (chiefly public) to purchase that work, and an organisation that gives them unity, confidence and a corporate identity.' But the final paragraph of the book counterbalances these remarks with a caveat:

> Seen in the perspective of history, the visual arts in Wales have made remarkable headway in the period since 1850, and all the existing conditions are propitious for further progress. However, not all the possible conditions are present, and so there are no grounds for complacency. Wales still has no national academy of art; there is neither a Welsh Museum of Modern Art, nor a Museum of Modern Welsh Art; and there has yet to appear a body of scholarship dedicated to the future as well as to the history of art in Wales.

And there you have it. Swings and roundabouts. With the lowest average earnings in Great Britain, and a culture which accords visual artists anything but privileged status, why do so many young artists decide to stay in or come to Wales? Artists are mobile by necessity rather than by nature, and their migratory patterns are chiefly determined by financial constraints. Artists have always been born in Wales, and have always visited Wales in search of subject matter, but what has made art in Wales increasingly conceivable and practicable has been the enlightened expenditure of public money on direct and indirect support for contemporary art and artists. In relatively recent years such support was focused largely through the Welsh Arts Council,

though there is no doubt that the upgrading and expansion of the art colleges at Cardiff and Newport during the 60s attracted as teaching staff to the area an influx of artists who made a sudden and significant difference to the profile of contemporary art in Wales, the effect of which persists.

At present, the Welsh Arts Council, the Institutes of Higher Education, three Welsh Regional Arts Associations, the Contemporary Art Society for Wales, the Welsh Sculpture Trust, the Association of Artists and Designers in Wales, the '56 Group Wales' (founded in that year but periodically inviting a number of artists under 40 to its fold), Gweled (the Welsh Language Society for the Visual Arts founded in 1984), increased local authority arts spending, various Welsh development agencies, twin towns, marina mania and a forthcoming national garden festival, between them offer to younger artists such attractions as grants, public art commissions, international exchanges, public exhibition spaces, studios, workshops, residencies, loans for artists and for purchasers of their work, and real communities within which to practise community art.

Some of the artists under 40 who went to art school in Wales within this climate of expectations found that the swings and roundabouts were a bit more difficult to climb on to than they had been led to believe. The Pioneers is a non-profitmaking working cooperative with a basic core of seven artists, supplemented as need be, who now busy themselves with exterior murals, play-structures and the like. Outside the localised repercussions (usually positive) of each of their projects, what excites most people about The Pioneers, more than what they do, is what they are and how they set themselves up. In 1981 five fine art graduates from Cardiff Art College were determined to break the apathetically sustained matrix of zero employment expectations by creating their own – this was before Enterprise Allowances and the full brunt of Thatcherism. Trying at first to run their own gallery, they were subsequently to concentrate on 'visual arts projects to improve the environment in Wales' so successfully that they are now used as a role model by other groups. However, the way they go about things, including their amusingly self-deprecatory annual report and press conferences, sets them apart from most community art groups – their administrator, after all, did 'train' to be a performance artist. With a large turnover, and even a small profit, are they now set to become another 'Public Art Agency', or will they remain The Pioneers?

Sculpture is particularly vigorous in Wales, and has been since *Arte Povera* and its funky American counterparts authorised artists to use scavenged and non-precious materials, particularly wood – and David Nash had a lot to do with that. Some younger sculptors who established such a profile during the 70s are still firmly based in Wales over a decade later.

Peter Ellis uses domestic bric-a-brac set in motion by small electric motors to make an unconventional form of low-tech kinetic sculpture. He was employing this sort of urban bricolage before or at least at the same time as the likes of Woodrow and

Ayers made a wrought-iron garden gate for the Liverpool Garden Festival, but is better known for his stone sculptures carved into convoluted but discrete forms with some of the resonance of folk art and neolithic rock engravings. He has undertaken several public commissions. Philip Chatfield has combined making his own studio-based sculpture with the employment of traditional stonecarving skills to make an extended series of commissioned commemorative panels integral to new housing in Swansea's maritime quarter. Chris Kelly is currently completing a large public bronze, comprising several groups of figures, commissioned for the 150th anniversary of the Chartist uprising in Newport, Gwent. Robert Kennedy, meanwhile, has subverted this spreading public sculpture mode with his *The Memorial,* an anti-war anti-monument made with genuine spleen and a few rude words which have upset a few people – a healthy sculptural corrective.

Emma Geliot and Deborah Jones are young sculptors who also make a lot of drawings as more than just an incidental activity. Emma Geliot's extravagantly informal sculptures are like 3-D realisations of her wild and ridiculous drawings, many of them about music and furniture. Deborah Jones' carved and assembled

L to R: Philip Nicol, *Waterfront*, 1985, acrylic; Emrys Williams, *Conversations Mid-Afternoon*, 1987-9, oil

Cragg, who are his contemporaries, and if Ellis' work has not gained as wide exposure as theirs it can only be because he has not been offered the right opportunities outside Wales in the right places at the right time. Flimsily insinuating or manically attention-seeking, Ellis' objects (let's not call them sculptures) transcend the simple joke and enter a different realm of subversive poetic silliness; they are original and genuinely popular. His recent static bronzes successfully transfer some of the same qualities to a quite different medium.

Consistently using unorthodox sculptural material such as paper pulp since before it became fashionable to do so, Lois Williams' work has a strong identity. Born in North Wales, but living outside Wales for some time, the experiences arising from her recent return have been reflected in her work. Dick Powell's sculptures made from thin sheets of coloured metal, often mounted on a springy base, are like crazy zoomorphic totems (he has also written and designed several sculptural theatre performances). His work is becoming less evidently stagey; it is getting leaner and sharper, and ought to be more widely seen.

Other younger sculptors in Wales are turning to the more traditional media of stonecarving and bronze casting. Alain

wooden sculptures seem to lead a different but parallel life to her more traditional but still unusual and highly accomplished drawings of animals. She was recently 'apprenticed' to Anna Maria Pacheco, thanks to a WAC 'Masterclass' grant.

Howard Bowcott and Michael Fairfax, in different ways, make exterior non-monumental sculptures from local materials, often for specific rural settings, *à la* David Nash. Howard Bowcott's recent work has been much influenced by his working visits to Zimbabwe, one thread in his work being the construction of large 'vessels' from such materials as North Wales slate, wood and moss growing in peat clods. Michael Fairfax's shrines and thrones are made from such ingredients as mixed woods, stone, copper wire and embroidery silks, in a delicate way not usually encountered in work intended for an outdoor setting.

Younger painters in Wales are representative of international pluralist trends rather than anything specifically Welsh, though their subject matter is often geographically particular. Emrys Williams (who has a London gallery, Benjamin Rhodes) paints static, strongly constructed and rather austere glimpses of unpeopled spaces (sometimes viewed through a car wing mirror) in the winter seaside town on the North Wales coast where he lives.

The scale of his canvases, and their confident handling, leads them away from the verge of mere repetition and makes them into something special, coming from an unexpected source. Philip Nicol, five years older, has employed a similar viscous paint surface in a series of large articulating canvases of gritty monumentality informed with an edge of irony, again articulating the sense of a specific place, the abandoned Cardiff docklands. The human figure is sometimes here, though in an absented, ghostlike way. Lately Nicol's work has been undergoing a period of reassessment, exploring traditional genres such as the still life and street scene.

Marion Thomson's dark paintings, on the edge of abstraction, also evoke the atmosphere of specific places in an individual and mature way, while Maggie James' poetic domestic interiors and Sally Moore's large dream paintings are 'interior' in both the literal and subjective sense without being wilfully self-indulgent, which is their strength. Quite different is Indra Khanna, whose prints and gouaches mix acute observation of the modern manners of her urban peers, with flights of fancy entirely her own. She is energetic, imaginative, and an artist to watch.

Michael Kelly, like Emrys Williams, is the sort of painter you

Once, believe it or not there was a Fluxus Festival at Aberystwyth University. But the heyday of performance art in Wales in over. Roland Miller is elsewhere, Marty St James and Anne Wilson have left Wales for London, the world and your TV screens, and Rob Conybear now makes sculpture for Swansea Maritime Quarter. But it is worth taking note of a closely related time-based trend which has been particular to Wales. Nonliterary theatrical performance, sometimes known as 'visual theatre', has been a very strong force in Wales, with such performance groups as Moving Being, Cardiff Lab, Paupers Carnival, and lately the radical Welsh language performance group Brith Gof (their recent stunning *Gododdin* production, in a great empty car factory in an urban no-man's-land on a windy evening, was surely performance art on a large scale), as well as specially commissioned new work by companies of high impact from outside Wales and abroad (Chapter Arts Centre in Cardiff is largely responsible for this). There is a crossover between this sort of work and that of visual artists, who have often been commissioned to collaborate with the companies mentioned above. Most recently, for example, Moving Being's *In Dusseldorf and Nebraska*, a project about Joseph Beuys and Gordon

L to R: Indra Khanna, *No-One Knows Herself*, 1988, gouache; Maggie James, *Kursters Ladder*, 1986, gouache

do not expect to encounter where you find him, seriously and effectively espousing a radical sort of traditionalism on the coast of West Wales, where artists are often concerned with servicing the tourist trade. You are even less likely to expect to find a Welsh-speaking former schoolteacher and adherent of Tàpies producing extraordinary work in a front bedroom in the Swansea valley. Ten years ago Frank Watkins was making savagely mystical tableaux representing archetypal spiritual symbols in the most base corporeal form possible, as some of the less acceptable examples of common urban waste. Since then his work has become much quieter and more muted, surfaces of apparent waste ground and fragments of friable detritus, consummately made on a paper base with plaster, paint and found objects (but nothing at all to do with Mark Boyle). Events on these surfaces are as infrequent as changes of stress in a musical composition by Arvo Paart, and with equally numinous impact if attended to. Following a brief exploratory period living in London, and a trip to meet Tàpies in Catalonia, made possible by the Elephant Trust's purchase of one of his works (subsequently donated to the Contemporary Art Society), Watkins is back in Wales, now making smaller mixed media works and collages.

McRae (who died on the same day), included a substantial sculptural input from performance artists Anne E Hayes and Glenn Davidson (who are aka Life Support System, for some years touring performances and workshops about perception and cognition inside a gigantic zoetrope).

This is a partial selection, viewed from the most populous corner of Wales, of some of its younger artists who have been most 'visible' of late. 'Visibility' is a problem for artists in Wales, not only across its difficult terrain, but especially beyond its borders. Some of the artists under 40 mentioned above are still in the process of establishing a place for their art in Wales. Some have already done so, and their work is well known within a Welsh frame of reference. But in either case all of these artists would probably admit to feeling 'invisible' within any wider context. There is no evidence of nascent Glasgow-style whizzkid artists in Wales, but more important is the fact that contemporary art from Wales has not achieved an identity akin to that of 'Scottish art'. The words 'Scottish art', however equivocal, do now at least evoke some *names*. We should be just as concerned with de-marginalising particular artists from Wales, as with establishing the Principality as an artistic territory.

CALUM COLVIN

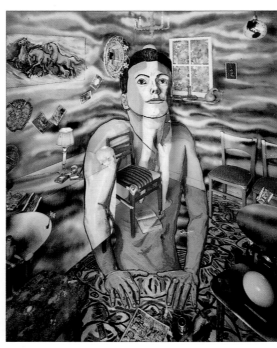

Garden of Earthly Delights, 1987, triptych. Colvin breaks down categories by assembling within a confined three-dimensional context a collection of objects combining fine art and kitsch – 'pictures with mirrors and icon-crowded sanctuaries' – which he photographs and then dismantles. By painting on real objects, he manipulates spatial dimensions, negating the depth between images from art history and consumer waste, dissolving the distinctions between art and life, and questioning values.

MICHAEL PETRY

Left: *Chaos Human Atomica: The Birth of the Parallel Universe*, 1988, installation. Viewers wear protective clothing for this investigation of 'parallel ideas of creation as interpreted by Science, Sex and Religion'. A central 'chandalier' contains 103 chemical elements in 103 test tubes, a video is shown on six monitors and reflected off the mirror-foil walls. *Right*: panel from *Parallel Works*, 1988, clothing folded sculpturally into picture frames and painted, suggestive both of wearer and art object.

RICHARD WILSON

Above: *Leading Lights*, February 1989, eclectic cable and light bulbs installation. *Leading Lights* was made in seven days on site at the Kunsthallen Brandts Klaedefabrik in Odense, Denmark, by using the lighting system of the gallery space as its material focus. The 84 lights in the ceiling space have been extended to one of the room's 12 windows and laid at rest in the space between the inner and outer glazing, creating a dense, bright white, glowing band. The light geometry and light energy of the room have been condensed and concentrated. The viewer feels the light and heat as he/she moves towards the window, its intensity burns the eye leaving an uncomfortable after image as you turn to look away. Overhead the lattices of strung cables become increasingly overlapped and plaited as they touch the vanishing point above the window to drop in a column of lines. A strange geometry is created from the lines to remind the viewer of the building's past history of looms weaving and spinning strands of wool. Unlike their previous position in the ceiling the cluster of bulbs sit on the window-sill like white-hot coals firing the base of the 'framed' chimney standing outside beyond the window. As the afternoon light diminishes so a part of the room begins to warm in the intense light at the window, picking out each overhead cable coming towards it. One senses the lines of air in the room, the clashing of man-made and natural as two sorts of light meet at the glazed division between outdoor and indoor, real and artificial (*see also Back Cover*). *Below*: *20:50*, August 1987, used sump oil and steel, installation at Royal Scottish Academy. This installation, originally installed at Matt's Gallery, transforms a waste material – used sump oil – into one of perfect purity and reflection. A steel walkway allows the viewer to seemingly walk through the oil.

ANDRE STITT

Nite Thoughts, Cornerhouse Manchester, 1987

DISPARATE POCKETS
(Or: How not to Paint Yourself into a Corner)
Simon Herbert

The immediacy, the active relationship with the viewer – the use of kitsch and horror tactics – and the dimension of time allow performance artists to comment on the human condition in ways unavailable to sculpture and painting. Simon Herbert, himself a video and performance artist, looks at the origins of live art and argues for its continual vigour as an artform, looking in particular at the work of André Stitt and Stephen Taylor Woodrow.

Informal conversation about performance art tends to echo a similar response to that of the Iran-Contra Scandal: everybody knows that something has happened, but exactly *what* and who should take the blame for it is only a matter for those interested enough to embark on an intensive investigation. However, the ghosts of performance actions prove resoundingly impervious to exorcism. In the re-telling of events, differing versions snowball like urban myths ('He was in the bath of offal for seven continuous days . . . or was it just eight straight hours . . . ?'), but they continue to intermittently puncture through the studied indifference of the mainstream artworld and the manic pop consumption of the general public. We all have our favourite Chinese whispers: Chris Burden, crucified on the roof of a Volkswagen, appearing briefly from a garage on Speeding Avenue; Gilbert and George, immobile and painted, singing 'Underneath The Arches'; Joseph Beuys locked in a cage with a wild coyote for seven days; Stuart Brisley fasting for ten days over Christmas, then crawling through the remains of profferred food.

An important by-product of performance, due to its transient nature, is the phenomenon of word-of-mouth. Yet amidst the myth there is – as in all myths – an element of selection that omits and distorts. The tacit assumption, voiced by so many critics for so many years, that performance art functions as an avant-garde King Arthur ready to emerge from misty slumber whenever the threat of cultural and social stagnation looms on the horizon is an appealing one, but is simply not true. It belies the fact that for the past four decades artists have been *continually* producing live work. They have been pushing forward and mutating the parameters of their practice regardless of the vagaries of an art infrastructure that only occasionally deigns to discover anew the bastard child.

One of the reasons for this consistency of activity is that performance art proffers an essential tool to the artist: the potential to share immediacy with the viewer in time and space through that most recognisable of symbols – the human form. It is therefore political by its very nature – and politics are part of the human condition. The genesis of performance art can be traced to the actions of the Cabaret Voltaire artists of 1916 Zurich. Artists such as Hugo Ball, Hans Arp and Tristan Tzara (conscientious objectors all) were horrified at the perversion of an industrial era which had not, as hoped, ushered in a period of liberation from the work ethic, but was used instead to mass-produce killing machines for the first global wars. Their perpetrations of nonsense actions were designed to outrage and (along with the later subconscious delvings of the Surrealists) sprang from a desire to spurn the conventional language and rhetoric of a corrupt social order. Their voice – however dated it may now appear – was the voice of rage.

In 1989, the targets of this voice have become more fractured and specific, and the work of contemporary performance artists has matured accordingly. There are no shortage of windmills to tilt at in a Britain which, like a punch-drunk boxer, blindly lashes out at the slightest allegation of internal rot, limping battered and bloodied into its colonial sunset. Our most notable export of late is the soccer thug. We fiddle on our filofaxes as the last of our North Sea Oil burns. The Bomb hangs over all our heads, making the notion of protest appear genetically redundant. Whilst such issues may not be explicit within the vast range of individual works by performance artists, they are *implicit*. To intervene is the birthright of the nuclear generation. Reports therefore of performance art's (literally) bloody birth(s) and death(s) have been greatly exaggerated, and there is a whole new generation of artists who need, in expressing themselves, to step outside the rhythms of conventional politesse.

One such artist is André Stitt. 30 years old, Stitt has been building up a large body of live work since 1976, when he studied at Belfast College of Art and Design. His engagement with performance art in many ways follows the 'classic' formula of a painter whose canvases became too limited to contain his energies. Instinctively rebellious against institutions (as he continues to be), his transition from the confines of product-based work to live work was helped when he came upon the work of Alistair Maclennan. Maclennan, now an internationally respected performance artist (who, in his capacity as head of the MA course in Belfast, has been responsible for a consistent emergence of time-based artists) was at the time embarking on a regular series of non-advertised street works.

> He was in the street, doing whatever he was doing, and he was getting noticed. Some people were laughing – he was getting a reaction. Afterwards I asked him why he was doing it, and he said that he wasn't sure why. That I should go out and set myself a target of one action a week. Set up a situation, and then bounce off it. Then ask yourself why you did that. And then do another.

Which Stitt did. Making 'akshuns' (as he calls them) culminated in a symbolic exorcism of his previous interest in painting by burning all his work in the college square – not exactly the most original action ever attributed to an artist but, accompanied by Stitt's daubing of the slogan ART IS NOT A MIRROR IT IS A FUCKING HAMMER, it signified a shift away form secure territories. In 1980, Stitt left Belfast and moved to London, precipitated by his perceptions of a hometown that he could no longer stand. The complexity of the situation in Belfast almost demands a response, yet he had always felt isolated on every level – in his art practice, with his family, sociologically. Instead he wanted the anonymity and objectivity that London offered. He says that he has only recently come to terms with this; although he regards himself as an Irish artist living in England, he is quick to react against peoples' expectations of such a 'responsibility'. In recent years, Stitt has occasionally worked collaboratively (most often with fellow Irish artist Tara Babel), yet in such situations he feels he tends to become dominant. Aware of this, he finds himself holding back.

This is certainly not the case in his solo work, His performances are invariably violent and cathartic, located within a multi-layered and complex world of low-art kitsch iconography. I first saw him perform in 1984 at the Projects Centre, Dublin. *Love Crimes* was a performance in which Stitt moved with conflicting forces of manic abandon and intense concentration through a series of structured scenarios on the theme of a drinking (and to large extent male) culture. Buffered by over-lapping slide and film projections, and punctuated by a relentlessly driving tacky backing track, he indulged in a compacted 'night on the town': sinuously disco-dancing whilst ketchup dribbled down him and trailed on to the floor, vomiting into a potty, manipulating a radio-controlled car that intermittently exploded condoms around the space, blowing fireballs into the audience.

The meanings in Stitt's work are not articulated through dogma. In *Love Crimes* and his other performances, his commentary evolves through a series of juxtapositions that refuse to be tidy or be pigeon-holed into single statements. The wreckage that remains at the end of his performances is part of the whole; it can be swept away, but not the vision of a world we normally prefer not to see. The visceral nature of such work begs the inevitable question – is Stitt merely trying to shock? It is a question he has obviously heard many times, one which he feels is too easy a response:

> It's a lot easier to shock in real life, if that's what I wanted to do. Sure there is a confrontation, because I want the audience to react, to experience, to say 'this is crazy'. So laugh at it, or shout at it. But don't just sit there. The audience has got to work just as hard as I do. That may sound pompous, but otherwise they won't get anything out of it. Every time I perform I'm frightened to death. Afterwards I maintain an initial high, then get terribly depressed. It's exhausting mentally, and my own assimilation of the work only connects months later, sometimes with small things that make me realise I've pin-pointed something.

The form of power that Stitt exerts over his audience is too considered to be written off as knee-jerk outrage. During his performances a sense of self-scorn is tangible. The element of threat is directed internally as well as externally. In this respect the viewer becomes both voyeur and narcissist, confronted with the desire to see Stitt push himself ever further. Whilst watching him eating dog food, wearing a Mickey Mouse hat, or shooting himself repeatedly in the head with blanks, we are forced to recognise our own emotional bankruptcy, our greed for visceral consumption. 'Life is incredibly complex. You have eyes, look at the incredible visions around you. It's not simple. What does that do, what language is that? What are the signs and symbols of how you articulate your life? Why do we spend so much money on things that we don't need.' Stitt is currently planning a tour of Texas, including venues at Houston, Austin and Dallas. He welcomes the prospect of returning to perform in the kitsch nation of the world, not least because audiences there seem more receptive to his work than British ones. He is very sceptical about the recently lauded new high profile for performance art, particularly conscious of the fact that his work is not easily appropriated into the support structure of municipal gallery-land: 'Where's the new support? I think interest comes and goes in waves. For myself I like to think that I've established some respect for what I'm doing, as I've built it up over the years. Most galleries would rather I didn't exist, but I won't give up or be put down. I never went away.'

29-year-old artist Stephen Taylor Woodrow's approach to performance is radically different from Stitt's both in form and content, yet he is faced with a similar challenge to maintain the integrity of his work. The reason, though, stems from its overt popularity. Over the last few years Taylor Woodrow has become one of the few British performance artists to regularly appear on the mainstream international art circuit. He has shown at the New York Museum of Contemporary Art and is currently touring Australia.

The 'springboard' for these activities was a performance first shown in 1986, *The Living Paintings*, in which he and three other performers became 'living art' by hanging on gallery walls (by use of a specially constructed, hidden harness). The work generated a response which far exceeded his expectations, and became a regular feature in the domain of commercial media coverage. Television appearances by *The Living Paintings* and extensively syndicated newspaper articles resulted in massive public attendance whenever they performed.

Amidst such a brouhaha, it is all to easy for an artist's intentions to be retroactively perceived as creating the work to precisely garner such a response. However, *The Living Paintings* is only one of numerous works that Taylor Woodrow has been steadily developing over the last few years. His entry into the arena of live work was a result of a number of factors: whilst studying at Goldsmiths' he realised that he found painting boring, he was introduced to the works of the Futurists and the European avant-garde (via Glen Baxter) and he decided that the computerised installations he was making at the time finally became redundant when he could do what they did himself. A group of like-minded colleagues became involved with Taylor Woodrow under the collaborative banner Club Boring. With the motto 'We Enlighten as we Entertain', they performed works such as *The Ubiquitous Biscuit* and its sequel *For a Few Biscuits More* (a Victorian melodrama/spaghetti western with only one recurring line 'The Custard Cream'). The performances were, despite appearances, anti-Bohemian, and gently ironic of popular romantic visions of the Artist:

> Ask anybody in the street what an artist is and they have very fixed ideas about what that person is. The artist as hero, starving in his loft. It might be romantic but it's not relevant in 1989. We're not all like Van Gogh. I am interested in the notion of the artist as an ordinary person.

Was it not curious, then, that in producing *The Living Paintings* he was locating himself centrally back within painterly trappings?

> Again, it's ironic. I did return for a while to making paintings, but I missed the response that I got from performing, I started to ask myself whether people enjoy anybody else's paintings more than a good performance. I came to the conclusion that they didn't. I attempted to make my paintings as interesting as my performances.

The harnesses that Taylor Woodrow and the other performers were strapped into became excrutiatingly painful and tiring over the long, sometimes eight-hour, durations. Taylor Woodrow adamantly discounts the suggestion that the Artist as Sufferer was a formal element of the work: 'No. Absolutely not. We try to make everything as comfortable as possible. Other artists would feel they needed to make the pain as obvious as possible. Build the harnesses out of barbed wire. It was the effect that was foregrounded, not the pain.'

Metaphysical discomfort was a central element of the 1988 piece *Going Bye Byes*: a number of hospital beds were lined along either side of the space. The beds were hollow and hid the performers' bodies, so that only their faces protruded claustraphobically from the pillow. Sterile and bleak, yet hypnotic at the same time, it illustrated a number of points Taylor Woodrow wanted to make:

The word populist has been used a lot about my work. That's not my intention, I think it's a dirty word. The work is popular not populist. I think I proved with *Going Bye Byes* that I could incorporate subject matter that is unpopular, yet at the Castle Museum in Nottingham, for instance, six thousand people saw the work in one day.

His latest project, currently being planned, will involve even more extensive choreography of performers. *The Birds* will feature 30 performers engaging in a 'large-scale bizarre situation'. Wearing specially constructed blackbird masks, but otherwise normally-dressed, the performers (amongst them children and old age pensioners) will gather in a city centre (Taylor Woodrow has gone so far as to plagiarise Hitchcock's original publicity 'The Birds *Is* Coming') and perform a series of pre-arranged mundane rituals ie standing on street corners, congregating in the nearest pub.

The Birds will be a structured event, but random elements will add to and shape it in terms of immediate public reactions (something Taylor Woodrow is interested in – when *Going Bye Byes* was shown at Bracknell Arts Centre somebody placed a live scorpion on one of the beds). *The Birds*, though, is a performance which Taylor Woodrow hopes will not particularly generate extensive media attention. However, he is realistic in recognising its uses:

Ten years ago coverage of performance art in this country

was virtually unheard of. I like to think that I've gone some way to break the ice. It can play a large part in helping to get support for future projects. That is not to say that all media coverage is a good thing. Trivialisation is something that I worry less about when I think that I've been making enough work over the last few years to dispel accusations of the 'jokey, one-off' (something that is more of a problem outside of Britain). It's a predictable reaction, lots of performers get it. It's partly because of performance art in general, partly against Stephen Taylor Woodrow as I'm an outsider in terms of the art world. As are many performance artists.

The work of Taylor Woodrow and Stitt is not – nor would they themselves claim it – definitive of the range of activities developing under the performance art umbrella. Neither would they especially lump themselves together in terms of their approach. The danger of melding artists' works together for the sake of an illustrational shorthand often arises when dealing with a relatively small pocket of art activity; such a view is insensitive, both to the unique qualities of artists' individualistic efforts, and to the potential eclectic range of the medium itself. What *is* evident in Taylor Woodrow's and Stitt's work is a commitment to continue to work within the live arena regardless of market forces. Which is why (and this may come as a surprise to some people) performance artists are here to stay.

STEPHEN TAYLOR WOODROW

L and R: The Living Paintings, 1986

Above L to R from 'New Contemporaries': Peter Kennelly, *Secret Thoughts*, 1988, acrylic, oil; Emma Lawton, *Sliding Sun*, oil, tissue paper; *Below L to R* from *New Talent*: Rufus Knight-Webb, *Breakwater*, 1988, acrylic; Sally Hall, *Big Fish*, 1988, oil

NEW CONTEMPORARIES, NEW TALENT
Young Artists at Auction and in the Gallery

Simon Gales, *Polyptych*, 1988, oil

The unprecedented interest in young artists, in finding new names, the opening of new galleries, and a commercial market for their work, is also shown in a number of recent events that would have been unheard of a few years ago: touring exhibitions of the work of recent graduates and the presentation of young artists at auction. Of these the most significant was the Christie's 'New Contemporaries' sale in March at the Royal College of Art.

Contemporary art at auction is a relatively recent phenomenon, a way of selling art away from the West End art gallery and where it is the public that determines the prices. (Alongside this are auctions where artists donate works to be sold in aid of a charity or political cause such as the recent 'Arts for the Earth' auctions on behalf of Friends of the Earth at Bonham's in London and Bearne's in Torquay.) 'New Contemporaries' featured works in a variety of styles and media by about 20 artists, many of whom, such as Simon Gales, Richard Webb and Claudia Morretti, have only recently graduated, and others such as Anita Taylor, John Bicknell and Marion Thomson who have exhibited widely but are unattached to commercial galleries. It gave a chance to see some of the talent emerging from art schools and, interestingly, that abstraction

(both expressionist and conceptual) as a trend featured as strongly as representative figuration and narrative. This is in interesting contrast to the work of most artists currently seen in commercial galleries, although also related to the interest in Conceptual Art shown by some participants in *Freeze*, and is perhaps a reflection that these artists are working independently and can continue to experiment, rather than having to produce in one particular style once it has been proved sellable or fashionable, as sometimes requested or pressurised by attachment to one gallery, and trends among buyers that determine that at the moment the figurative and the symbolic are 'in'. This freedom is something perhaps lost when artists are taken on as soon as or even before they graduate and was also recognised by the curators of the exhibition *New Talent*, who deliberately included some works they considered 'unresolved'.

Selected by Sir Hugh Casson, Isobel Johnstone and artist Stephen Farthing, the exhibition, *New Talent*, at Winchester Gallery represented the outcome of a competition open to artists working in southern Britain who graduated as recently as 1985-7. The aim was to discern the emergence of new talent among young artists as yet unrecognised by influential

dealers and critics, but perceived as 'possible true survivors' in the contemporary artworld, 'an expanding market . . . welcoming the appearance of relatively accessible up-to-date art'. In the catalogue introduction, Johnstone discusses the problems confronting such young artists, the pressures to conform to critical categories and the struggle to establish an individual artistic identity immediately discernible to critics and buyers, who are increasingly turning their attention to the work of very young artists. In contrast to 'New Contemporaries' and *Freeze* representing the more avant-garde trends in contemporary art, *New Talent* was dominated by more traditional figurative and expressionist concerns among the artists exhibited (only one of whom is abstract, although two combine abstraction and landscape): 'Stories are being told, modern allegories devised and passions aroused . . . Most subscribe to an expressionist approach, indulging in a search for self-expression.' The exhibition aimed to provide viewers with an insight into this search for an artistic identity by including some unresolved paintings, revealing the difficulties involved in the creative process, and reflecting the current interest among dealers and critics in the early work and development of better-known artists.

This checklist is a first attempt at compiling a list of exhibiting artists under 40. It is hoped to extend and amend the list as more information is received; please address any contributions to the Checklist Editor, Art & Design, Academy Group Ltd, 42 Leinster Gardens, London W2 4AN. We give here only minimal information including where possible major exhibitions and present galleries where appropriate. Galleries are in London unless otherwise stated.

VICTORIA ACHACHE
(abstract painter, Berkeley Square Gallery) Born 1952, studied Byam Shaw. Selected exhibitions: 1987 solo Stephen Bartley Gallery, 1988 *Three Abstract Painters* Berkeley Square Gallery

JANE ACKROYD
(sculptor, Anderson O'Day) Born London 1957, studied St Martin's and RCA. Solo exhibitions: 1985 Kingsgate Workshops Gallery, 1988 Anderson O'Day

STEVEN ADAMSON
(sculptor) Selected exhibitions: 1988 *Freeze*

SAM AINSLEY
(painter/collage constructor) Born Tyne and Wear 1950, studied Leeds, Newcastle Poly (fine art) and Edinburgh (tapestry). Selected exhibitions: 1987 solo Third Eye Centre Glasgow, group *Vigorous Imagination New Scottish Art* Scottish National Gallery of Modern Art

EDWARD ALLINGTON
(sculptor, Lisson Gallery) Born Westmorland 1951, studied Lancaster and Central, lives and works London. Solo exhibitions: 1986 Galerie Adrien Maeght Paris, Galerie Montenay-Delsol Paris, Galerij S65 Belgium, Diane Brown New York, 1987 Diane Brown New York, Marlene Eleini London

SIMONE ALEXANDER
(painter) Born 1964 London, lives London. Selected exhibitions: 1988 *Open Futures* Ikon Gallery Birmingham

PETER APPLETON
(environmental sculptor) Born 1955, lives Exeter. Recent landscape-sculpture exhibited at Arnolfini, *A Noise In Your Eye* and artist-in-residence in Forest of Dean

SALEEM ARIF
(painter, Anderson O'Day) Born India 1949, studied Birmingham and RCA. Selected exhibitions: 1987 group Whitechapel, Serpentine Gallery, Air Gallery, 1988 solo Anderson O'Day

CAROLINE ASSHETON
(painter, Albemarle Gallery) Born 1961, studied Camberwell and City & Guilds, lives and works London. Selected exhibitions: 1989 solo Albemarle Gallery

KEVIN ATHERTON
(environmental sculptor) Born 1950, lives London. Work in Forest of Dean, Brixton Railway Station and Stoke-on-Trent Garden Festival

JOHN ATKIN
(sculptor) Born Darlington 1959, studied Leicester Poly and RCA, lives and works London. Selected exhibitions: 1986 solo Juda Rowan Gallery, group Basle Art Fair, *Recent British Sculpture* Hong Kong, 1987 Athena Awards Barbican, *Hackney Artists Drawings* Charlotte Street Gallery, City Artists Gallery

DAVID AUSTEN
(painter, Anthony Reynolds Gallery) Born Essex 1960, studied Maidstone and RCA. Solo exhibitions: 1986 and 88 Anthony Reynolds Gallery, 1987 Serpentine Gallery, 1988 Arnolfini Bristol

ALAIN AYERS
(Sculptor) Born Dartford 1952, studied Exeter and Birmingham, 1987 Travel Award to China, lives and works Cardiff. Member *56 Group Wales*. Selected exhibitions/commissions: 1987 sculpture for Holm View Leisure Centre Barry, 1988 *Stoneworks* Powis Castle

STEPHEN BARCLAY
(painter, Raab Gallery) Born Ayrshire 1961, studied Glasgow, lives and works Scotland. Exhibitions: 1987 solo London, 1989 *The New British Painting* Cincinnati

MARIE BARBOUR
(printmaker) Born Irvine 1963, studied Glasgow, lives and works Glasgow. Solo exhibitions: 1986 McLean Museum and Art Gallery Greenock, 1988 Arnolfini Council Touring Gallery

INIGO BATTERHAM
(painter, Albemarle Gallery) Born 1958, studied Camberwell and Goldsmiths. Solo exhibitions: 1986 Gallery 24, 1988 Albemarle Gallery

TORIE BEGG
(painter) Studied City & Guilds and Central, lives and works London. Solo exhibitions: 1987 and 89 Sue Williams Gallery, 1987 Louise Hallett Gallery

REZA BEN GAJRA
(mixed-media painter) Born Mauritius 1962, studied Central, Bath and Chelsea. Selected exhibitions: 1986 group Cornerhouse Manchester, 1987 group Chisenhale Gallery, 1988 solo Freuds Wine Bar, Pleasance Gallery Edinburgh

PAUL BENJAMINS
(painter, Thumb Gallery) Born London 1950, studied Camberwell and RCA. Solo exhibitions: 1985-7 International Contemporary Art Fair London and Los Angeles, Bath Contemporary Art Fair, Galerie Pascal Gabert Paris

TONY BEVAN
(painter, Matt's Gallery) Born 1951, studied Bradford, Goldsmiths and Slade. Selected exhibitions: 1987-8 ICA solo touring, group *Cries and Whispers* British Council touring, 1988 solo Ronald Feldman Gallery New York, Gallery Wittenbrink Munich, group *Aperto* Venice Biennale, 1989 Haus Der Kunst Munich

ZARINA BHIMJI
(photographer/mixed-media artist) Born 1963, currently post-graduate Slade. Selected exhibitions: 1989 *The Essential Black Artist*, 1989 *Big is Beautiful* V&A Museum

JOHN BICKNELL
(painter) Born Surrey 1958, studied North-East London Poly and Slade. Selected exhibitions: 1986 group Camden Arts Centre, Fundació Joan Miró Barcelona, solo Carlile Gallery, 1988 group Whitechapel Gallery

LOUISE BLAIR
(painter, Nicola Jacobs Gallery) Born Kent 1958, studied Canterbury, Hornsey and Chelsea, lives and works London. Solo exhibitions: 1986 and 89 Nicola Jacobs Gallery

ELIZA BONHAM CARTER
(painter, Berkeley Square Gallery) Born London 1961, studied Cambridge College of Art and Technology, Ravensbourne and RCA, Abbey Major Scholarship/Prix de Rome. Selected exhibitions: 1988 group Paton Gallery, *Three Abstract Painters* Berkeley Square Gallery

HOWARD BOWCOTT
(environmental sculptor) studied Newcastle Univ, lives and works North Wales, two working visits to Zimbabwe. 1988 first prize Criccieth Festival Sculpture Show.

SONIA BOYCE
(painter pastels and collage) Born London 1962, Studied East Ham and Stourbridge, lives and works London. Solo exhibitions: 1986 Black Artists Gallery, Air Gallery, 1988 Whitechapel Art Gallery

PHILIP BRAHAM
(painter) Born Glasgow 1959, studied Duncan of Jordanstone Dundee and Royal Academy of Fine Art in The Hague, lives and works Edinburgh. Solo exhibitions: 1987 Glasgow Arts Centre, 1988 The Scottish Gallery, 1989 Raab Gallery London

GILLIAN BRENT
(sculptor, Yorkshire Art Space Society) Born Bedfordshire 1959, studied Wimbledon and St Martin's, lives and teaches Sheffield, involved in community projects. Selected exhibitions: 1987 group Sheffield Festival, 1988 solo Worcester City Art Gallery, group *Intercity 88* Visual Arts Festival Birmingham and Sheffield

MARTYN BREWSTER
(painter, Thumb Gallery) Born Oxford 1952, studied Brighton Poly. Selected exhibitions: 1987 solo Woodlands Art Gallery, group Thumb Gallery, Int Contemp Art Fair Los Angeles

DAVID BROCK
(painter/sculptor) Born 1966, studied West Surrey and Liverpool Poly. Selected exhibitions: 1988 Bluecoat Gallery Liverpool, 1989 New Academy Gallery

GLEN BROWN
(painter, oil plus photos) Born 1966, studied Norwich and Bath. Selected exhibitions: 1987 *Art Matters* Winchester College of Art, 1988 Contact Gallery Norwich

HUGO BRUTTON
(painter and printmaker, Long & Ryle) Born London 1959, studied London College of Printing, Falmouth and Chelsea. Selected exhibitions: 1986 Angela Flowers Gallery, 1987 London Printmakers Council, Athena Art Awards Barbican, 1988 Long & Ryle

PAVEL BUCHLER
(photographer) Born Prague 1952, living in Britain since 1981. Solo exhibitions: 1988 Third Eye Centre Glasgow

ANGELA BULLOCH
(sculptor/installation artist) Born Ontario, Canada 1966, studied Taunton and Goldsmiths, lives and works London. Selected exhibitions: 1986 St Paul's Arts Centre Oxford, 1988 *Freeze*

FRANCES BURDEN
(painter, Paton Gallery) Born Wakefield Yorkshire 1964, studied Wakefield, Canterbury and Slade. Selected exhibitions: 1988 *New Faces* Paton Gall, Elizabethan Gallery Wakefield

RUTH CALLAND
(painter, Paton Gallery) Born Scunthorpe 1963, studied Lincolnshire, Lanchester Poly and Chelsea. Selected exhibitions: 1986 *New Contemporaries* ICA, National Garden Festival Stoke-on-Trent, 1987 *Three Figurative Painters* Paton Gallery

STEVEN CAMPBELL
(painter, Raab Gallery) Born Glasgow 1953, studied Glasgow, lives and works Glasgow. Selected exhibitions: 1986 solo Raab Galerie Berlin, Galerie Pierre Huber Geneva, John Berggruen Gallery San Francisco, 1987 solo Marlborough Fine Art, group British Council touring, 1989 *The New British Painting* Cincinnati

FIONA CARLISLE
(painter, 369 Gallery Edinburgh) Born Wick, Scotland 1954, studied Edinburgh, lives Greece. Solo exhibitions: 1986 369 Gallery Edinburgh, 1988 Barbican

ANDREW CARNIE
(painter/sculptor) Born London 1957, studied zoology/psychology Durham University, art Goldsmiths and RCA, lives and works London. Selected exhibitions: 1986 London Contemporary Art Fair, Carnie Chaple Gallery, 1987 Angela Flowers, 1988 Zanzibar Club, Whitchapel Open, Giray London

ANN CARRINGTON
(sculptor) Studied RCA

HELEN CHADWICK
(video/performance artist) Born Croydon 1953, studied Brighton Poly and Chelsea, lives and works London, 1987 shortlisted Turner Prize. Selected exhibitions: 1987 group Birmingham City Museum & Art Gallery, Third Eye Centre Glasgow, Mappin Art Gallery Sheffield; 1989 Marlene Eleini Gallery, *Enfleshings* book, event Whitechapel Gallery and exhibition Interim Art, *Big is Beautiful* and *Photography Now* V&A Museum

SIMON CHALMERS
(photographer/installation artist). Selected exhibitions: 1988 Riverside Open, Otis Gallery Wapping

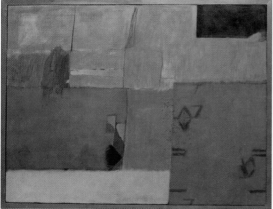 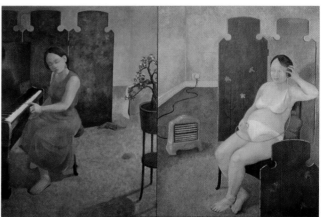

L to R: Victoria Achache, *The Red Carpet*, 1987-8, oil; Ruth Calland, *Untitled*, 1987, oil

STEPHEN CHAMBERS
(painter, Angela Flowers Gallery) Born 1960, studied St Martin's and Chelsea. Selected exhibitions: 1987 solo Winchester Gallery, group Angela Flowers Gallery, 1988 solo Bluecoat Gallery Liverpool, Jenny Todd Gallery, group Nigel Greenwood Gallery, Flowers East

PHILIP CHATFIELD
(sculptor) Born Southsea 1958, studied Newcastle Univ, lives and works Wales. Selected exhibitions: 1986 Glynn Vivian Art Gallery Swansea, 1988 *Stoneworks* Powis Castle, 1989 stone-carvings commissioned for Swansea Maritime Quarter

SUE COE
(painter) Born England 1951 lives and works New York. First major exhibition in Britain: 1989 Museum of Modern Art Oxford

ALEXANDER COLLINS
(abstract painter) Born 1965, studied Portsmouth and Bath, lives and works Hampshire. Selected exhibitions: 1987 *Art Matters* Winchester School of Art

HANNAH COLLINS
(photographer, Matt's Gallery) Born 1956 London, studied Slade, scholarship to USA, lives and works London. Solo exhibitions: 1986 Matt's Gallery, 1987 Ikon Birmingham, commission for Hacienda club Manchester, 1988 't Venster Gallery Rotterdam, group *Aperto* Venice Biennale, 1988-9 *Matter of Facts* French touring exhibition, 1989 *Big is Beautiful* and *Towards a Bigger Picture* V&A Museum. Book *Legends*, published 1988 by Matt's Gallery/ICA

NIAMH COLLINS
(Anderson O'Day) Born Dublin 1956, studied Portsmouth Poly and RCA. Selected exhibitions: 1986 Grafton Gallery Dublin; 1987 South London Art Gallery, Anderson O'Day

MATTHEW COLLISHAW
(photographer/installation artist) Born Nottingham 1966, studied Trent Poly and Goldsmiths. Selected exhibitions: 1988 London Institute of Education, *Freeze*

CALUM COLVIN
(artist/photographer, Salama Caro Gallery) Born Glasgow 1961, studied sculpture Duncan of Jordanstone Dundee and photography RCA, lives and works London. Selected exhibitions: 1987 group Photographers Gallery, 1987 solo Seagate Gallery Dundee, 1989 Salama Caro Gallery

STEPHEN CONROY
(painter) Born Helensburgh 1964, studied Glasgow. Selected exhibitions: 1986 solo Dunbarton District Council, 1987 group Royal Scottish Academy Edinburgh, Washington Gallery Glasgow, Turberville Smith London, 1989 *The New British Painting* Cincinnati

RICHARD CONWAY JONES
(painter and film-maker, Long & Ryle) Born at sea 1964, studied Berkshire and Harrow. Selected Exhibitions: 1987 Dance Attic Putney, 1988 Wargrave Art Gallery, *Assemblages* Brixton Brasserie

CHRISTOPHER COOK
(painter and poet, Benjamin Rhodes Gallery) Born Yorkshire 1959, studied Exeter (art), Exeter Univ (English/art) and RCA. Solo exhibitions: 1987 Galliva Maggiore Bolgone, 1988 Benjamin Rhodes Gallery, 1989 Cleveland Gallery Middlesbrough, Plymouth Arts Centre, Benjamin Rhodes Gallery

DAVID COOK
(painter) Born Dunfermline 1957, studied Duncan of Jordanstone Dundee. Solo exhibitions: 1987 Ancrum Gallery Roxburghshire, 369 Gallery Edinburgh, Flaxman London, 1989 369 Gallery Edinburgh

ANDREW COOMBES
(painter oil and charcoal) Born 1962 London, studied Amersham, Camberwell and Univ of Ulster, works Belfast and Dundonald. Selected exhibitions: 1988-9 *Irland-Deutschland Exchange*

EILEEN COOPER
(painter, Benjamin Rhodes Gallery) Born Derbyshire 1953, studied Goldsmiths and RCA, lives and works London. Selected exhibitions: 1987 solo Artsite Bath 1988 solo Benjamin Rhodes Gallery, 1989 *The New British Painting* Cincinnati, 1989 Benjamin Rhodes

TONY CRAGG
(sculptor, Lisson Gallery) Born Liverpool 1949, studied Wimbledon and RCA, lives and works Dusseldorf, 1988 Turner Prize. Selected exhibitions: 1987 group Hayward Gallery, Galerie Kanransha Tokyo, Marian Goodman Gallery New York, 1988 solo British Pavilion Venice Biennale, 1989 group *British Sculpture 1960-1988* Museum van Hedengaagse Kunst Antwerp

FRANK CREBER
(painter, Sue Williams Gallery) Born 1959, studied Univ of Newcastle and Chelsea. Selected exhibitions: 1987 group RCA, Smith's Gallery, Sue Williams

GRAHAM CROWLEY
(painter) Born Romford 1950, studied St Martin's and RCA, lives and works Cardiff. Selected exhibitions: 1989 *The New British Painting* Cincinnati

KEN CURRIE
(painter, Raab Gallery) Born North Shields 1960, studied Glasgow, lives and works Glasgow. Selected exhibitions: 1987 group Serpentine Gallery, Nicola Jacobs Gallery, Turberville Smith, 1988 solo Raab Gallery Berlin and Third Eye Glasgow, 1989 *The New British Painting* Cincinnati

ANTHONY DALEY
(painter, Angela Flowers Gallery) Born Jamaica 1960, studied Chelsea. Selected exhibitions: 1986 solo Angela Flowers Gallery, group Commonwealth Institute, 1987 Angela Flowers, Turnpike Gallery Manchester, 1988 solo Angela Flowers

DEXTER DALWOOD
(painter, Paton Gallery) Born Bristol 1960, studied St Martin's and Baroda University. Selected exhibitions: 1986 *Three British Artists* Bombay and New Delhi, solo Paton Gallery

IAN DAVENPORT
(painter, Waddington Galleries) Born Kent 1966, studied Goldsmiths, lives and works London. Selected exhibitions: 1985 Whitworth Art Gallery Manchester, 1988 *Freeze*, Karsten Schubert

GRENVILLE DAVEY
(sculptor, Lisson Gallery) Born Launceston 1961, studied Goldsmiths, lives and works London. Selected exhibitions: 1988 *Aperto* Venice Biennale

MERISSA DAVIES
(painter, Albemarle Gallery) Born 1962, studied Dublin, Taunton, Cheltenham and RCA, lives and works Bristol. Selected exhibitions: 1986 Axiom Art Gallery Cheltenham, 1987 *London Art Schools*, Brussels, 1988 *Art Al Fresco* Royal Academy, 1989 Albemarle Gallery

RICHARD DEACON
(sculptor, Lisson Gallery) Born Bangor, Wales 1949, studied Somerset College, St Martin's and RCA, lives and works London, 1987 Turner Prize. Solo exhibitions: 1986-7 Galerie Arlogos Nantes, *For Those Who Have Eyes* Aberystwyth Arts Centre and touring, 1987-8 Lisson Gallery travelling exhibition Maastricht, Lucerne, Madrid, Antwerp, 1988 Lisson Gallery, Marian Goodman Gallery New York, 1988-9 Whitechapel Art Gallery

GRAHAM DEAN
(painter large watercolours, Austin Desmond Fine Art) Born Birkenhead, Merseyside 1951, studied Bristol Poly. Solo exhibitions: 1987 Basle Switzerland, Artsite Bath, 1988 Austin Desmond Fine Art, 1989 Nerlino Gallery New York

JEFFREY DELLOW
(painter, Todd Gallery) Born 1949, studied St Martin's, Maidstone and Slade, teaches Humberside. Selected exhibitions: 1987 solo Castlefield Gallery Manchester, 1988 group Todd Gallery, Athena Art Award, Whitechapel Open

DOMINIC DENIS
(painter) Selected exhibitions: 1988 *Freeze*

JOHN DEVANE
(painter, Paton Gallery) Born Blackpool 1954, studied Blackpool, Liverpool and RCA. Selected exhibitions: 1987 *London Group* RCA, 1988 two-person Paton Gallery

WILLIE DOHERTY
(photo artist) Born Derry 1959, studied Ulster Poly, lives and works Derry. Selected exhibitions: 1987 *A Line of Country* Cornerhouse Manchester, 1988 solo Third Eye Centre Glasgow, solo Oliver Dowling Gallery Dublin, Battersea Arts Centre, 1988-9 *Matter of Facts* (French touring exhibition), *Irland-Deutschland Exchange*

MICKY DONNELLY
(painter and printmaker) Born Belfast 1952, studied Queen's Univ Belfast, Ulster Poly, British School Rome, lives and works Belfast. Selected exhibitions: 1987 solo Newry and Mourne Arts Centre, Arts Council Gallery Belfast and Orchard Gallery Derry, 1988 group *Cries and Whispers* (British Council touring), solo Taylor Galleries Dublin, Third Eye Glasgow, 1988-9 group *Irland-Deutsch-*

land Exchange

STEPHEN DOWSING
(video/installation/performance artist) Born 1953, studied (printmaking) Liverpool Poly. Selected exhibitions: 1988 AVE Festival Arnhem, 1989 *Video Positive* Tate Liverpool

CHRIS DRURY
(environmental sculptor/installation) Solo exhibitions: 1989 Orchard Gallery Derry

PHILIP DUTHIE
Born Aberdeen 1957, studied Gray's Aberdeen. Solo exhibitions: 1986 369 Gallery, 1988 Collective Gallery Edinburgh

SIMON EDMONDSON
(painter, Nicola Jacobs Gallery) Born London 1955, studied City & Guilds, Kingston and Syracuse New York. Selected exhibitions: solo 1986 Michael Haas Gallery Berlin, Turske and Turske Gallery Zurich, Nicola Jacobs, Lang and O'Hara New York, 1987 Nicola Jacobs Gallery, 1989 David Beitzel Gallery New York, group *The New British Painting* Cincinnati

KATHARINE EDWARDS
(painter) Born 1963, studied St Martin's and Ecole des Beaux-Arts Paris, lives and works Herefordshire. Selected exhibitions: 1987 group Gallery des Beaux-Arts Paris, 1988 group *Art for Youth* Mall Galleries, 1988 and 89 solo The Wine Gallery

FELIM EGAN
(painter/mixed-media artist) Born Strabane 1952, studied Ulster Poly, Portsmouth Poly, the Slade, British School Rome, works Dublin and Edinburgh. Selected exhibitions: 1988-9 *Irland Deutschland Exchange*

PETER ELLIS
(sculptor) Born Manchester 1950, studied Manchester, Wolverhampton and Chelsea, livee and works Cardiff, member *56 Group Wales*. Selected exhibitions: 1987 *Springing to Life* Manchester City Art Gallery, Artists Bath, 1989 Andrew Knight Gallery Cardiff, Mostyn Gallery Llandudno.

MICHAEL FAIRFAX
(Sculptor) Born Windsor 1953, studied Portsmouth and Newport Gwent. Selected commissions: 1987 Blackbays Sussex, Common Ground

ANGUS FAIRHURST
(painter) Born Kent 1966, studied Canterbury and Goldsmiths, lives and works London. Selected exhibitions: 1988 *Progress by Degree* Bloomsbury Galleries, *Freeze*

TIM FARGHER
(painter, Long & Ryle) Born 1952, studied St Martin's. Selected exhibitions: 1986 Aldeburgh Festival of Music and the Arts

GILLIAN FARMER
(painter) Born 1962 Bannockburn, studied Falkirk and Glasgow, works Glasgow. Solo exhibitions: 1988 Alloa Museum, 1989 369 Gallery Edinburgh

STEPHEN FARTHING

L to R: Richard Conway Jones, *Ivy (No 6)*, 1988, oil; Grenville Davey, *Purl*, 1988, painted steel

(painter, Edward Totah Gallery) Born London 1950, studied St Martin's and RCA, lives and works London. Solo exhibitions: 1986 Edward Totah Gallery, 1987-8 Museum of Modern Art Oxford and Edward Totah Gallery. Hayward Gallery Artist-in-Residence Jan-April 89

AMANDA FAULKNER
(painter, Angela Flowers Gallery) Born Dorset 1953, studied Bournemouth, Ravensbourne and Chelsea, lives and works London. Selected exhibitions: 1986 solo Angela Flowers Gallery, group Scottish Arts Council, 1987 Serpentine Gallery, Angela Flowers, Artsite Gallery Bath, 1988 Lefevre Gallery, 1989 *The New British Painting* Cincinnati

STEPHEN FINER
(painter, Berkeley Square Gallery) Solo exhibitions: 1986 and 88 Anthony Reynolds Gallery

CHRIS FISHER
(painter and tapestry maker) Born 1950, studied Winchester, St Martin's and RCA, lives and works London. Selected exhibitions: 1988 *Exhibition Road* RCA

DENZIL FORRESTER
(painter) Born Grenada 1956, studied Central and RCA, late 1'960s worked London, now lives New York. Selected exhibitions: 1986 solo Commonwealth Institute, 1988 group *Exhibition Road* at RCA

KAREN FORSYTH
(painter, Albemarle Gallery) Born Aberdeen Scotland 1953, studied Oxford (D Phil Richard Strauss and Hofmanstahl). Selected exhibitions: 1987 group Raab Gallery London, solo Barbican Centre and Chicago International Art Fair (Raab Gallery), 1989 solo Albemarle Gallery

MARK FRANCIS
(painter) Born 1962, studied St Martin's and Chelsea, lives and works London. Selected exhibitions: 1986 group Paton Gallery, London Institute Show Royal Festival Hall

SIMON FRASER
(painter, poet, printmaker, 369 Gallery Edinburgh) Born Inverness 1950, studied Ruskin, Grays, official artist Arctic Lapland Exhib 1973, works Nairn. Solo exhibitions: 1986 Artspace Aberdeen, 1988 369 Gallery Edinburgh

CHLOE FREEMANTLE
(painter, Berkeley Square Gallery) Born London 1950, studied Byam Shaw, lives and works London and New York. Selected exhibitions: 1987 solo Sue Rankin Gallery, group Kenkeleba House *Current Thinking* New York

STUART FROST
(environmental sculptor) Born 1960, studied RCA, lives London, 1986 artist-in-residence Forest of Dean

PAUL FURNEAUX
(painter, Todd Gallery) Born Aberdeen 1962, studied Edinburgh. Selected exhibitions: 1987-8 group Compass Gallery, Open Eye Gallery, Backroom Gallery, Fruitmarket Open Edinburgh, 1989 solo

Todd Gallery

SIMON GALES
(painter) Born 1965, studied Ipswich and Goldsmiths. Selected exhibitions: 1988 *New Realists* Berkeley Square Gallery, The Group Show Battersea

ANYA GALLACCIO
(sculptor/installation, Anderson O'Day) Born Glasgow 1963, studied Kingston and Goldsmiths. Selected exhibitions: 1987 group Farnham, 1988 *Freeze* , *Poetic Figuration in the 80s* Lauderdale House, 1989 group Anderson O'Day.

EMMA GELIOT
(sculptor) Studied Cardiff, lives and works Cardiff. Selected exhibitions: 1988 Cardiff Visual Arts Festival

ROSE GIBBS
(painter) Born 1965, studied Chelsea, currently post-graduate at Chelsea.

RICHARD GILBERT
(painter casein and tempera, Raab Gallery) Born Plymouth 1957, studied Falmouth, Wimbledon, Chelsea and British School Rome, currently Harkness Fellowship to Chicago. Selected exhibitions: 1988 and 89 Raab Gallery, 1988 Chicago Exposition, LA Art 88

TRICIA GILLMAN
(painter, Benjamin Rhodes Gallery) Born Johannesburg, South Africa 1951, studied Univ of Leeds and Newcastle. Solo exhibitions: 1985 Arnolfini, Benjamin Rhodes Gallery, 1987 Benjamin Rhodes

JUDITH GODDARD
(installation/video artist) Born 1956, studied Reading and RCA. Selected exhibitions: 1989 *Video Positive* Tate Liverpool

ANDY GOLDSWORTHY
(enviromental sculptor, Fabian Carlsson Gallery) Born Cheshire 1956, lives and works Dumfrieshire, 1987 artist-in-residence Yorkshire Sculpture Park, 1988 projects in Japan, USA, Denmark, Holland, France and Italy, 1989 projects in USA, France and the Arctic

ANTONY GORMLEY
(sculptor – moulds from own body) Born London 1950, studied anthropology Cambridge Univ, art Central, Goldsmiths and Slade, lives and works London. Selected exhibitions: 1987 solo Salvatore Ala New York, Serpentine Gallery, *Drawings* Siebu Contemporary Gallery Tokyo, group *Avant-Garde in the 80s* Los Angeles, 1988 *Starlit Waters* Tate Liverpool, *The Impossible Self* Winnipeg Canada, 1989 solo Louisiana Museum Denmark and the Scottish National Gallery of Modern Art.

ROBERTA GRAHAM
(photographer) Born Londonderry, Northern Ireland 1954, studied West Surrey and North East London Poly. Solo exhibitions: Arnolfini Bristol, Orchard Gallery Derry, 1989 *Big is Beautiful* V&A Museum

ROBERT GRAVER

Born 1963, studied Chelsea and RCA. Selected exhibitions: 1988 show of constructions at London College of Furniture

ADAM GRAY
(painter, Anderson O'Day) Born London 1963, studied St Martin's. Solo exhibitions: 1987 and 89 Anderson O'Day

PETER GRIFFITHS
(painter, Yorkshire Art Space Society) Born Loughborough 1960, studied Loughborough and Brighton, lives and works Sheffield. Selected exhibitions: 1989 solo Huddersfield Art Gallery, two-person Wakefield District College

JON GROOM
(painter, Nicola Jacobs Gallery) Born Powys 1953, studied Cardiff, Sheffield and Chelsea, 1987-8 artist-in-residence Villa Valdberta Munich. Solo exhibitions: 1986 and 88 Nicola Jacobs Gallery, 1987 Edition E Munich, 1988 Lorenzelli Arte Milan

ALEXANDER GUY
(painter, Paton Gallery) Born St Andrews 1962, studied Duncan of Jordanstone Dundee and RCA. Selected exhibitions: 1986 solo Seagate Gallery Dundee, 1987 group Riverside Open, London Group RCA

GWEN HARDIE
(painter and sculptor, Paton Gallery) Born Newport Fife 1962, studied Edinburgh, lives and works West Berlin. Selected exhibitions: 1987 solo Fruitmarket Gallery Edinburgh, group *Vigorous Imagination* Scottish National Gallery of Modern Art, 1988 solo Paton Gallery, Kettle's Yard Cambridge, 1989 *The New British Painting* Cincinnati

RICHARD HARRIS
(sculptor) Born Devon 1954, studied Torquay and Gloucester, 1978-81 and 87 working in Australia. Selected exhibitions/commissions 1982-6 Bottle Bank commission for Gateshead, 1989 *British Sculpture 1960-88* Museum van Hedendaagse Kunst Antwerp

VANDA HARVEY
(painter/printmaker) Born 1957, studied Kingston, North East London and Brighton Poly. Selected exhibitions: 1988 *Printed Matter* Smith's Gallery, *Printmaking Survey* Brighton Museum.

WILLIAM HARVEY
(painter, Sue Williams Gallery) Born Hampshire 1957, studied Birmingham Poly. Solo exhibitions: 1987 Lanchester Gallery Coventry, 1988 Sue Williams Gallery

MONA HATOUM
(video/performance/installation artist) Born Beirut Lebanon 1952, studied Beirut, Byam Shaw and Slade, lives and works London. Residence 1986-7 Chisenhale Dance Space, performances *Edge 88*

JAMES HAWKINS
(painter)Born Reading 1954, studied Wimbledon, Worthing, Ruskin, works Ullapool. Solo exhibitions: 1986 Maclean Museum Greenock, 1987 Torrance Gallery Edinburgh, 1987 Eden Court Inverness, 1988 369 Gallery Edinburgh

SALLY HEYWOOD
(painter, Paton Gallery) Born 1964, studied Gloucester (painting fellow 1987/88). Selected exhibitions: 1988 group *Aspects of Landscape* Paton Gallery, 1989 two-person Paton Gallery. Youngest artist to have work in 20 C-coll of MOMA, NY

NICOLA HICKS
(sculptor, Angela Flowers Gallery) Born London 1960 studied Chelsea and RCA, lives and works Hackney. Solo exhibitions: 1986 Angela Flowers, 1987 Beaux Arts Gallery Bath, 1988 Flowers East

DAMIEN HIRST
(painter/sculptor) Born 1965, studied Jacob Kramer College Leeds and Goldsmiths, lives and works London. Selected exhibitions: 1987 two-person Old Court Gallery Windsor, *Whitworth Young Contemporaries*, 1988 solo Old Court Gallery Windsor, two-person The Crypt Holborn, curated and exhibited in *Freeze*

DAVID HOSIE
(painter, Raab Gallery) Born Glasgow 1962, studied Edinburgh, lives and works Edinburgh. Selected exhibitions: 1987 solo Raab Gallery, 1988 group *The Rape of Europe* Galeria Gian Ferrari Milan, *Metropolis* Raab, *Lion Rampant: New Scottish Painting* Artspace San Francisco, Fruitmarket Edinburgh

SHIRAZEH HOUSHIARY
(sculptor, Lisson Gallery) Born Shiraz Iran 1955, studied Chelsea, lives and works London. Selected exhibitions: 1987 Lisson Gallery, *Current Affairs: British Painting and Sculpture in the 80s* Museum of Modern Art, Oxford, 1988 first major exh at Centre d'Art Contemporain Geneva (touring to Oxford 1989)

MICHAEL HOWE
(painter and sculptor). Born London 1963, studied Central. Selected exhibitions: 1983 *Young Blood* Barbican London, 1989 Wilson Hale Gallery

PETER HOWSON
(painter, Angela Flowers Gallery) Born London 1958, studied Glasgow, lives and works Glasgow. Selected exhibitions: 1987 solo Washington Gallery Glasgow, Angela Flowers, *Vigorous Imagination* Scottish National Gallery of Modern Art, 1988 solo The Scottish Gallery, Angela Flowers, 1989 group *The New British Painting* Cincinnati

IAN HUGHES
(painter, Raab Gallery) Born Glasgow 1958, studied Duncan of Jordanstone Dundee, lives and works Edinburgh. Selected exhibitions: 1987 solo 369 Gallery Edinburgh, group *Vigorous Imagination* Scottish National Gallery of Modern Art, 1988 monoprints Raab Gallery

GARY HUME
(painter, Karsten Schubert) Born Kent 1962, studied Chelsea, Liverpool Poly and Goldsmiths, lives and works London. Selected exhibitions: 1988 group *Freeze*, Karsten Schubert

JUDY INGLIS
Born Cornwall 1952, studied Exeter, Sheffield Poly

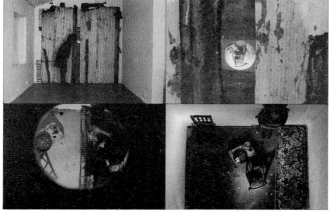
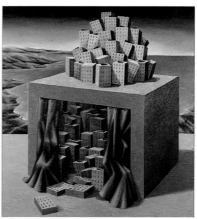

L to R: Mona Hatoum, *Matters of Gravity*, 1987, Riverside Studios, photographs; David Hosie, *Boxed Up*, 1988, oil

and RCA. Selected exhibitions: 1987 Birch and Conran Gallery, Gloucester College of Art, Cheltenham, Oxford Gallery Oxford, Smith's Gallery, 1988 Sue Williams Gallery

FRED INGRAMS
(painter, Albemarle Gallery) Born 1964, studied Camberwell and St Martin's (expelled for being 'disruptive'). Selected exhibitions: 1987 group Christopher Hull, Birch and Conran, Diarorama Gallery, 1988 solo Albemarle Gallery

CALLUM INNES
Born 1962 Edinburgh, studied Grays Aberdeen and Edinburgh. Solo exhibitions: 1986 Artspace Edinburgh, 1988 369 Gallery Edinburgh

MOIRA INNES
(sculptor/installation artist) Born Edinburgh 1957, studied Edinburgh, lives and works Edinburgh. Solo exhibitions: 1987 Third Eye Centre Glasgow, Richard Demarco Gallery Edinburgh

PHILIP INWOOD
(painter, Berkeley Square Gallery) Born 1959, studied Bath Academy. Selected exhibitions: 1987 solo Original Picture Shop, group Mercury Gallery

OLIVIA IRVINE
(painter) Born Ayrshire 1960, studied Edinburgh, lives and works Edinburgh. Solo exhibitions: 1987 WASPS Edinburgh, 1989 369 Gallery Edinburgh

MAGGIE JAMES
(painter) Born Cardiff 1956, studied Cardiff, Newcastle and RCA, lives and works Cardiff, member of *56 Group Wales*. Selected exhibitions: 1988 Andrew Knight Gallery Cardiff.

GAVIN JANTJES
(painter) Exhibition: 1989 *Contemporary Art by Black artists* 198 Gallery

CECILE JOHNSON
(sculptor, Nicola Jacobs) Born 1957, studied Cardiff, Ghana and Goldsmiths. Selected exhibitions: 1986 Greenwich Theatre Gallery, 1987 Acme Open Studios, 1989 Kunstverein Koln

ALISON JONES
(painter, Todd Gallery) Born 1962, studied at Goldsmiths and Slade. Selected exhibitions: 1987 solo Oxford Gallery, 1988 group Todd Gallery

DEBORAH JONES
(sculptor) Studied Cardiff, lives and works Cardiff. Selected exhibitions: 1988 Cardiff Visual Arts Festival.

LUCY JONES
(painter) Born London 1955, studied Camberwell and RCA. Selected exhibitions: 1986 group Angela Flowers, Solomon Gallery, 1987 solo Spitalfields Health Centre in assoc with Whitechapel Art Gallery, Angela Flowers Gallery, 1988 group *Exhibition Road* RCA

MIKE JONES
(video artist) Born 1962, studied Trent Poly. Selected exhibitions: 1989 *Video Positive* Tate Liverpool (with Simon Robertshaw)

EITHNE JORDAN
(painter, Paton Gallery) Born Ireland 1954, studied Dun Laoghaire School of Art. 1986 Guinness Peat Award. Selected exhibitions: 1989 two-person Paton Gallery

CLAIR JOY
(painter, Nicola Jacobs Gallery) Born Vancouver 1958, studied St Martin's and Goldsmiths. Solo exhibitions: 1987 Interim Art, 1988 Nicola Jacobs Gallery, Cornerhouse Manchester

ROD JUDKINS
(painter, Thumb Gallery) Born 1956, studied RCA. Selected exhibitions: 1987 solo Thumb Gallery, group 1985-7 International Contemporary Art Fair, London and Los Angeles, Bath Contemporary Art Fair, Redfern Gallery, Artsite Bath

FRANCOISE KAFFIN
(painter mixed-media) Born Rouen France 1962, studied Sheffield and Goldsmiths.

ANISH KAPOOR
(sculptor, Lisson Gallery) Born Bombay, India 1954, studied Hornsey and Chelsea, lives and works London. Solo exhibitions: 1986 Kunstnerses Hus Oslo, Barbara Gladstone Gallery New York, Albright Knox Art Gallery Buffalo, Univ of Massachusetts, 1987 Ray Hughes Gallery Sydney, 1988 Lisson Gallery

AARON KASMIN
(painter, Albemarle Gallery) Born 1963, studied Chelsea. Solo exhibitions: 1987 Gallery 24, 1988 Albemarle Gallery

JOHN KEANE
(painter, Angela Flowers Gallery) Born Hertfordshire 1954, studied Camberwell. Selected exhibitions: 1986 and 88 solo Angela Flowers Gallery, 1989 group *The New British Painting* Cincinnati

CHRISTOPHER KELLY
(sculptor) Born 1960, studied Leeds and Cardiff, lives and works Cardiff, 1986 artist-in-residence Elan Valley Visitor Centre Powys. Recent commissions: Powys Sculpture Trail and Newport Borough Council public sculpture

MICHAEL KELLY
(painter) Lives and works Dyfed Wales. Selected exhibitions: 1987 Nicholas Treadwell Gallery.

ROBERT KENNEDY
(sculptor) Born Liverpool 1963, studied Cardiff, lives and works Cardiff. Solo exhibitions: 1986 commission for Sculpture Wall Chapter Cardiff, 1988 *The Memorial* Chapter Cardiff, 1989 Aberystwyth Arts Centre

PETER KENNELLY
(painter) Born London 1965, studied Loughton and Goldsmiths. Selected exhibitions: 1988 *Eight Young Artists* Lauderdale House, 1989 Leicestershire Schools Art

BERNADETTE KERR
(painter, Todd Gallery) Studied Slade. Selected exhibitions: Todd Gallery

INDRA KHANNA
(painter and printmaker) Born 1960, studied Cardiff and Chelsea, lives and works Cardiff. Selected exhibitions: 1986 group Andrew Knight Gallery Cardiff, 1987 solo Plymouth Art Centre, 1988 solo Colston Hall Bristol, 1989 group Printmakers Council

RICHARD KIDD
(painter) Born Newcastle 1952, studied Newcastle Univ and British School Rome. Selected exhibitions: 1987-8 Mayor Rowan Gallery

JOANNA KIRK
(painter, Nicola Jacobs Gallery) Born Cheshire 1963, studied Goldsmiths. Solo exhibitions: 1987 Third Eye Centre Glasgow, Nicola Jacobs Gallery, 1988 Whitechapel Art Gallery, 1989 Carine Campo Gallery Antwerp

ANSEL KRUT
(painter, Fischer Fine Art) Born Cape Town, South Africa 1959, studied RCA. Selected exhibitions: 1984 solo Shell Gallery Johannesburg, John Moore's Liverpool Exhibitions XIV, IBM South Bank London, 1986 *Twelve British Artists* Kunstlerhaus Vienna

PETER KUHFELD
(painter, Agnew's) Born 1952 Cheltenham, studied Leicester Poly and Royal Academy Schools, lives and works Kent. Solo exhibitions: 1986 New Grafton Gallery, 1989 Agnew's

ALISON LAMBERT
(painter oils and charcoal, Long & Ryle) Born 1957, studied Lanchester Poly, lives and works Coventry. Selected exhibitions: 1986 Stoke-on-Trent Festival, 1987 solo Creaser Gallery

MICHAEL LANDY
(installation artist, Karsten Schubert) Born London 1963, studied textiles Loughborough and fine art Goldsmiths. Selected exhibitions: 1987 Bonner Showroom, 1988 Fre*eze*, Karsten Schubert, Riverside Studios

ABIGAIL LANE
(sculptor) Selected exhibitions: 1988 *Freeze*

JANE LANGLEY
(painter) Born London 1959, studied Chelsea, Camberwell, RCA and Cité International des Arts Paris. Solo exhibitions: 1986 The Oxford Gallery Oxford, 1986 and 89 Galerie Hilger Vienna

WILLIAM LATHAM
(computer artist) Born 1961, studied Ruskin Oxford, RCA and City of London Poly, lecturing and research Middlesex Poly, St Martin's, IBM Winchester. Selected exhibitions: 1986 solo Christ Church Oxford, 1988 group Riverside Studios, Whitechapel Art Gallery

EMMA LAWTON
(painter) Born 1962, studied Bristol Poly and Byam Shaw. Selected exhibitions: 1988 Open Studios SAAC Cardiff, *The Women's Festival* New County Hall Cardiff

CHRISTOPHER LE BRUN

(painter, Nigel Greenwood Gallery) Born Portsmouth 1951, studied Slade and Chelsea. Selected exhibitions: 1985 solo Nigel Greenwood, Fruitmarket Gallery Edinburgh, Arnolfini Bristol, 1986 solo Kunsthalle Basle, 1987 group *Avant-Garde in the 80s* Los Angeles

JOHN LEACH
(painter) Born Kent 1956, studied Brighton Poly. Selected exhibitions: 1985 Whitechapel Open

DAVID LEAPMAN
(painter, Todd Gallery) Born London 1959, studied St Martin's and Goldsmiths. Selected exhibitions: 1987 group Curwen Gallery, 1988 solo Todd Gallery and Ikon Gallery Birmingham, group Riverside Studios

ELZPIETA LEPA
(sculptor, Long & Ryle) Studied Cheshire and Birmingham, lives and works Birmingham. Selected exhibitions: 1986 solo Artsite Bath, 1987 group Atkinson Gallery Southport

STEPHEN LITTMAN
(video artist) Born 1957, studied Coventry Poly and RCA. Selected exhibitions: 1989 *Video Positive* Tate Liverpool

SARAH LUCAS
(sculptor) Born London 1962, studied Working Men's College, London College of Printing and Goldsmiths. Selected exhibitions: 1986 Showroom Gallery, 1988 *Freeze*

TOMMY LYDON
(painter/installation artist) Born Glasgow 1955, studied Glasgow. Solo exhibitions: 1987 Third Eye Centre Glasgow, 1989 Todd Gallery

MARY MABBUTT
(painter, Paton Gallery). Born Luton 1951, studied Luton, Loughborough and Royal Academy Schools. Selected exhibitions: 1986 Paton Gallery, 1987 *Six Figurative Painters* Paton Gallery, 1989 *The New British Painting* Cincinnati

ROB MCCARTHY
Born 1957 London, studied Hornsey and Edinburgh, works Edinburgh. Selected exhibitions: 1988 group *Art in General* New York, Piers Arts Centre Stromness, Kellie Lodging Fife, 1989 solo 369 Gallery Edinburgh

JOCK MCFADYEN
(painter) Born Paisley Scotland 1950, studied Chelsea, part-time lecturer Slade, 1985 artist-in-residence National Gallery. Selected exhibitions: 1988 Camden Arts Centre, 1989 *The New British Painting* Cincinnati

DAVID MACH
(installation artist) Born Methil Fife 1956, studied Duncan of Jordanstone Dundee and RCA. Selected exhibitions: 1986 solo *Fuel for the Fire* Riverside Studios, *If you go down to the woods* Cornerhouse Manchester, 1987 group *Vigorous Imagination* Scottish National Gallery of Modern Art, 1988 solo Nicola Jacobs Gallery, *101 Dalmations* installation Tate Gallery, 1989 *Tamed Trained Framed* Brussels

L to R: Michael Landy, *Astra*, 1988, pvc and clips; Moira Innes, *Untitled*, 1987, installation

KEITH MCINTYRE
(painter, Raab Gallery) Born Edinburgh 1959, studied Duncan of Jordanstone Dundee, lives and works Edinburgh. Selected exhibitions: 1986 solo 369 Gallery Edinburgh, group Compass Gallery Glasgow, 1987 *Vigorous Imagination* Scottish National Gallery of Modern Art, solo Raab Gallery Berlin, 1988 solo Raab Gallery London

LUCY MACKENZIE
(painter, Fischer Fine Art) Born Sudan 1952, studied Bristol Poly and RCA. Selected exhibitions: 1985 solo Coe Kerr Gallery New York, 1988 group *Exhibition Road* RCA

HARRY GREGORY MCKEOWN
(painter, Sue Williams Gallery) Born Dundee 1965, studied Central and St Martin's. Selected exhibitions: 1987 The Institute Gallery, The London Group Show, Henry Moore Gallery, 1988 solo Sue Williams Gallery

ROBERT MACLAURIN
(painter, 369 Gallery Edinburgh) Born 1961, studied Edinburgh, lives Edinburgh, works Edinburgh and Turkey. Solo exhibitions: 1987 Mercury Edinburgh, 1988 St Catherine's College Cambridge, 1989 369 Gallery Edinburgh

CAROLINE MACNAIRN
(painter, 369 Gallery Edinburgh) Born 1955 Selkirk, studied Edinburgh, lives and works Edinburgh. Solo exhibitions: 1986 Trevelyan College Univ of Durham, 1987 Le Cadre Hong Kong, 369 Gallery Edinburgh

BARRY MAGUIRE
(painter) Born Bray Co Wicklow 1951, studied Dun Laoghaire, National College Dublin, worked Italy and West Germany, lives and works Dublin. Selected exhibitions: 1988-9 *Irland-Deutschland Exchange*

ANTONI MALINOWSKI
(painter, installation, performance, Mario Flecha Gallery) Born Warsaw Poland 1955, studied Warsaw Art Academy and Chelsea, teaches Chelsea. Solo exhibitions: 1985 and 88 Wilma Tolksdorf Hamburg, installation/performances: 1986 The Drawing Room, 1987 Chisenhale, Riverside, Islington City Arts Festival

YVETTE MARTIN
(environmental sculptor) Born 1963, studied Loughborough, lives Loughborough, artist-in-residence Forest of Dean

SHAHEEN MERALI
(batik and collage artist) Born Tanzania 1959, moved to London 1970, studied Gwent, lives and works London, 1986 founded One Spirit Gallery and Batik Workshop. Selected exhibitions: 1988-9 group 198 Gallery, 1989 solo Tom Allen Community Arts Centre

LALA MEREDITH-VULJA
(photographer) Selected exhibitions: 1988 *Freeze*

NEIL METZNER
(painter) Born 1965, studied Harrogate and Chelsea. Selected exhibitions: 1988 Riverside Open, The Arthouse Show

KATHARINE MEYNELL
(video and performance artist) Born 1954, studied Byam Shaw and RCA. Selected exhibitions: Arts Council *Video Makers on Tour*, Genlock London Video Arts touring, 1989 *Video Positive* Tate Liverpool

ALAIN MILLER
(painter, Anthony Reynolds Gallery) Born 1961 London, studied Maidstone, Chelsea and Goldsmiths, works London. Solo exhibitions: 1987 Anthony Reynolds

JOANNA MILLETT
(video artist/film-maker) Born 1955, studied Maidstone and RCA, member of Hull Time Based Arts. Selected exhibitions: 1989 *Video Positive* Tate Liverpool

LISA MILROY
(painter, Nicola Jacobs Gallery) Born Vancouver Canada 1959, studied the Sorbonne, St Martin's and Goldsmiths. Selected exhibitions: 1988 solo Nichola Jacobs Gallery, 1989 solo Third Eye Glasgow, 1989 group *New British Painting* Cincinnati

ANN MONAGHAN
(painter, sculptor, collage) Studied Northern Ireland Poly, Wolverhampton and Chelsea, lives and works London. Selected exhibitions: 1988 *Open Futures* Ikon Gallery Birmingham

CATHY DE MONCHAUX
(sculptor) Born 1960, lives and works London. Solo exhibitions: 1985 Winchester Art Gallery, 1988 Mario Flecha Gallery, Angela Flowers (artist of the day)

PANDORA MOND
(painter, Gallery 10) Born London 1964, studied Ruskin Oxford, lives and works London. Solo exhibitions: 1984 and 1989 Gallery 10

JOHN MONKS
(painter, Paton Gallery) Born Manchester 1954, studied Liverpool and RCA. Selected exhibitions: 1985 solo Paton Gallery, 1987 *Six Figurative Painters* Paton Gallery, 1989 *The New British Painting* Cincinnati

JAMES MOONEY
(painter) Born Scotland 1955, studied Edinburgh, RCA and British School Rome, lives and works Edinburgh and London. Selected exhibitions: 1988 *Exhibition Road* RCA

SALLY MOORE
(painter) Born 1962, studied South Glamorgan, Ruskin Oxford and Birmingham Poly. Selected exhibitions: 1986 group *Direct Contact* Stuttgart/Cardiff exchange, 1988 group Dudley Art Gallery, Open Studios Glever St Birmingham, Talking Point Gallery Fishguard

TONY MOO-YOUNG
(painter/stained-glass, 198 Gallery) Born 1957, lives and works London, teaches Brixton College. Selected exhibitions: 1988-9 198 Gallery

HOWARD MORGAN
(painter, Agnew's) Born North Wales 1949, studied Newcastle Univ, lives and works London. Solo exhibitions: 1984 *Jazz Paintings* Claridges, 1988-9 Agnew's

CLAUDIA MORETTI
(painter) Born 1966, studied Heatherley's, Norwich and Chelsea, lives Richmond Surrey. Selected exhibitions: 1988 New Art.Centre

ANNE MORRISON
(painter) Studied Glasgow.

JOUMANA MOURAD
(painter, Raab Gallery) Born Manchester 1954, studied Heatherley's and Byam Shaw, lives and works London. Selected exhibitions: 1988 solo Raab Gallery, group Chicago International Arts Exposition, LA Art Fair, 1989 *Art 89* Business Design Centre

MICHAEL MULCAHY
(painter and formerly performance artist) Born Cork 1952, studied Crawford Cork and National College Dublin, studies in Africa, Polynesia and Australia, works from Dublin. Selected exhibitions: 1988-9 *Irland-Deutschland Exchange*

MICHAEL MURFIN
(painter, Piccadilly Gallery) Born 1954, studied Leicester, Trent and Birmingham Polys. Selected exhibitions: 1986 Piccadilly Gallery, Harlow Playhouse, 1988 Imperial College

DAVID MUTASA
(sculptor) Born Zimbabwe 1955, moved to England 1986, lives and works London. 1988-9 *The First Child* commission by Lambeth Council. Selected exhibitions: 1988-9 198 Gallery

STEPHEN NELSON
(painter, Mario Flecha Gallery) Born 1961, studied South Glamorgan Institute, Birmingham Poly, Ecole de Beaux Arts Nantes, lives and works London. Selected exhibitions: 1985 solo Axion Gallery Cheltenham, 1989 two-person Mario Flecha

THOMAS NEWBOLT
(painter, Browse & Darby) Born London 1951, studied Camberwell, scholarships to Italy, France and United States. Selected exhibitions: 1986 and 88 Browse & Darby, 1988 Tatischeff Gallery New York

JOHN NEWLING
(sculptor, Edward Totah Gallery) Born Birmingham 1952, studied Chelsea. Solo exhibitions: 1987 Jollenbeck Gallery Cologne, Edward Totah Gallery, 1988 California State University Los Angeles

PHILIP NICOL
(painter) Born Caerphilly 1953, studied Cardiff, lives and works Cardiff, member of *56 Group Wales*. Solo exhibitions: 1985 Andrew Knight Gallery Cardiff, 1988 Glynn Vivian Art Gallery Swansea

NELL NILE
(works in chalk on paper) Born 1949, lives and works Bristol. Solo exhibition: 1988 Arnolfini Gallery Bristol

LUCIA NOGUEIRA
(painter, Mario Flecha Gallery) Born 1950 Brazil, studied Chelsea and Central, lives and works London. Selected exhibitions: 1988 solo Carlisle Gallery, group Riverside Studios, Mario Flecha, 1989 *Promises, Promises* Serpentine Gallery

SIMON NORTH
(painter) Born 1955 Cheltenham, studied Edinburgh Univ and Edinburgh, lives and works Edinburgh. Solo exhibitions: 1988 Anta Spitalfields

TINA O'CONNELL
(painter and sculptor) Born 1964 Limerick, studied Limerick and Chelsea. Selected exhibition: 1988-9 *Irland-Deutschland Exchange*

MARCEL O'CONNOR
(painter, 369 Gallery Edinburgh) Born 1958 Co Armagh, studied Liverpol Poly, Brighton Poly and Cyprus College of Art, works in Edinburgh. Solo exhibitions: 1987 Collective Gallery Edinburgh, 1988 369 Gallery Edinburgh, 1989 Maclaurin Art Gallery Ayr, Gardner Arts Centre Univ of Sussex

HUGHIE O'DONOGHUE
(painter, Fabian Carlsson) Born Manchester 1953, studied Goldsmiths. Solo exhibitions: 1986 Fabian Carlsson Gallery London, Chapter Gallery Cardiff, Galleria Carini Florence, 1987 National Gallery artist-in-residence

RON O'DONNELL
(artist-photographer, Raab Gallery) Born Stirling 1952, studied Stirling Univ and Napier College Edinburgh, lives and works Edinburgh. Selected exhibitions: 1986 (with Calum Colvin) Photographers' Gallery, 1987 *Vigorous Imagination* Scottish National Gallery of Modern Art, 1989 Raab Berlin

SUZANNE O'DRISCOLL
(painter, Anderson O'Day) Born 1955, studied Central and Slade. Solo exhibitions: 1984 Air Gallery, 1987 Anderson O'Day

JULIAN OPIE
(sculptor, Lisson Gallery) Born London 1958, studied Goldsmiths, lives and works London. Solo exhibitions: 1986 Gallerea Franco Toselli Milan, 1986 and 88 Lisson Gallery

GILLIAN ORD
(painter) Born Middlesborough 1955, studied Winchester and Manchester Poly. Two-person exhibition 1989 Wilson Hale Gallery

THERESE OULTON
(painter, Marlborough Fine Art) Born Shrewsbury 1953, studied St Martin's and RCA, lives and works London. Solo exhibitions: 1986 Galerie Thomas Munich, Galerie am Moritzplatz Berlin, 1988 Marlborough Fine Art, Hirschl & Adler New York

SIMON PACKARD
(printmaker, Long & Ryle) Born Sunderland 1960, studied Brighton Poly and RCA (printing). Solo exhibition: 1988 Turnpike Gallery Leigh

STEPHEN PARK

L to R: Shaheen Merali, *Unilever Strike*, 1988, batik; Hughie O'Donoghue, *Crows II*, 1988, oil

(sculptor) Born Edinburgh 1962, studied Newcastle, Goldsmiths and Slade, Boise scholarship 1987, lives and works London. Selected exhibitions: 1983 *New Contemporaries* ICA, 1988 *Freeze*

CORNELIA PARKER
(environmental sculptor) Born Cheshire 1956, studied Gloucester, Wolverhampton and Reading, lives and works London. Selected exhibitions and commissions: 1986 National Garden Festival Stoke-on-Trent, Siteworks Project London, 1987 solo Actualities, 1988 Forest of Dean Sculpture Project

EMILY PATRICK
(painter, Agnew's) Born 1959 Kent, studied architecture Architectural Association and Cambridge Univ. Solo exhibitions: 1986 and 1989 Agnew's

RICHARD PATTERSON
(painter) Born 1963, studied Watford and Goldsmiths, lives and works London. Selected exhibitions: 1988 *Freeze*

SIMON PATTERSON
(conceptual painter) Born Surrey 1967, studied St Albans and Goldsmiths. Selected exhibitions: 1988 *Freeze*, 1989 solo Third Eye Centre Glasgow

ASHLEY PEARCE
(painter, Sue Williams) Born London 1962, studied Lancashire Poly. Selected exhibitions: 1987 Doncaster Art Gallery, Manchester City Art Gallery, The Garden Gallery, Peterborough Museum and Art Gallery, Sue Williams, 1988 Mall Galleries, Kettle's Yard Cambridge

SIMON PERRY
(sculptor, Nicola Jacobs Gallery) Born London 1962, studied Croydon, Chelsea and Royal Academy Schools, 1986 RA gold medal for sculpture, 1987 Prix de Rome scholarship sculpture. Solo exhibition: 1988 Nicola Jacobs Gallery

CLAUDIA PETRETTI
(painter) Studied Edinburgh.

MICHAEL PETRY
(multi-media performance/installation artist) Born Texas USA, lives and works London. Selected works: 1987 *Deceptions* performance for *National Review of Live Art* Riverside Studios, 1988 *International Monument to the Unknown Citizen* Slaughterhouse Gallery, *Chaos Human Atomica* Unit 7 Gallery, *Parallel Works* Adam Gallery

BERNARD PLANTEROSE
(painter, 369 Gallery Edinburgh) Born 1956 London, studied Eastborne, ecology Edinburgh Univ, lives and works Duartbeg Scotland, painting and managing nature reserves. Solo exhibitions: 1987 369 Gallery Edinburgh, Eden Court Theatre Inverness

DICK POWELL
(sculptor/performance) Studied Cardiff. Selected exhibitions: 1986 solo *Underwater Reign* Chapter Cardiff, 1987 group *Metal and Motion* Brighton Museum & Art Gallery

KATHY PRENDERGAST
(sculptor/installation artist) Born Dublin 1958,

studied National College of Art Dublin and plus work as video cameraperson, lives and works London. Selected exhibitions: 1988 *Open Futures* Ikon Gallery Birmingham

REBECCA PRICE
(painter and set designer) Born 1966, studied Slade. Selected exhibitions: 1988 Slade Group Show Bloomsbury Theatre, Slade Exhibition Space, Blenheim Gallery

SARAH RAPHAEL
(painter, Agnew's) Born 1960, studied Camberwell. Solo exhibitions: 1985 Christopher Hull Gallery, 1989 Agnew's

FIONA RAE
(painter) Born Hong Kong 1963, studied Croydon and Goldsmiths. Selected exhibitions: 1988 Freeze, 1989 Anderson O'Day

PETER RANDALL-PAGE
(environmental sculptor) Born Essex 1954, studied Bath Academy and marble carving in Italy. Selected exhibitions and commissions: 1987 *7th International Small Sculpture Exhibition* Budapest, 1988 commission at Chineham for European Year of the Environment, Forest of Dean Sculpture Project, New Milestones Project Dorset

JUNE REDFERN
(painter) Born Fife 1951, studied Edinburgh, lives and works London, 1986 artist-in-residence National Gallery. Selected exhibitions: 1986 solo National Gallery, group Fabian Carlsson, Mercury Gallery, 1987 *Vigorous Imagination* Scottish National Gallery of Modern Art, 1988 solo Mercury Gallery

CATHERINE REFORD
(painter) Born 1953, studied Canterbury and Royal Academy Schools. Selected exhibitions: 1986 open studio Acme Studios, group Showroom Bethnal Green, 1988 open studio Milbourn St Studio

PAUL RILEY
(painter, Berkeley Square Gallery) Born 1963, studied Bournemouth and Gloucester, currently at Royal Academy Schools. Selected exhibitions: Curwen Gallery, Bankside Gallery

MARY ROBERTS
(illustrator) Born London 1956, studied St Martin's, works London. Group exhibitions: 1985/6/7 *European Illustration* Royal Festival Hall, *Images* Smith's Gallery, 1988 *New Decorative Art* Harrods

TESSA ROBINS
(3-D mixed-media artist) Born 1965, studied Hertfordshire, Winchester and Middlesex Poly.

DONALD RODNEY
(mixed-media artist using X-rays as ground material for work) Born 1961, studied Bournville Birmingham, Trent Poly and Slade, 1988 residency Graves Art Gallery Sheffield. Selected exhibitions: 1987 group *State of the Art* ICA, *Depicting History* Mappin Art Gallery Sheffield, 1989 solo Chisenhale Gallery

NIGEL ROLFE

(sculptor/performance artist) Born Isle of Wight 1950, lives Dublin. Performance *Edge 88*

ANDREW ROSS
(painter) Born 1955, studied Lancaster Poly and RCA. Selected exhibitions: 1986 and 87 Royal Academy Summer Shows, 1988 Riverside Open

LUCY ROSS
(painter, Sue Williams Gallery) Born Edinburgh 1961, studied Wimbledon and RCA, 1987 studio in Paris. Selected exhibitions: 1986 solo Arcade Gallery Harrogate 1988 group Bankside Gallery, Sue Williams Gallery, Smiths Gallery, 1989 solo 369 Gallery Edinburgh

SARA ROSSBERG
(painter, Thumb Gallery) Born Peckinghausen West Germany, studied Academy of Fine Art Frankfurt and Camberwell. Selected exhibitions: 1986 Int Art Fair Basle, 1987 Kunstkeller Berne, Nicholas Treadwell Gallery, Int Contemp Art Fair Los Angeles

MARIO ROSSI
(painter, sculptor, printmaker, Anderson O'Day) Born Glasgow 1958, studied Glasgow and RCA, lives and works London. Selected exhibitions: 1987 solo Cleveland Gallery Middlesborough, group *Vigorous Imagination* Scottish National Gallery of Modern Art, 1988 solo Anderson O'Day

VERONICA RYAN
(sculptor) Born Montserrat 1956, studied Bath and Slade. Selected exhibitions: group 1986 *From Two Worlds* Whitechapel Art Gallery, 1987 solo touring Wolverhampton, Arnolfini Bristol and Third Eye Glasgow, 1988 two-person Kettle's Yard Cambridge

SOPHIE RYDER
(sculptor, Berkeley Square Gallery) Born 1963, studied Kingston and RCA, artist-in-residence 1986 Grizedale Forest, 1987 Salisbury Cathedral. Solo exhibitions: 1987 Edward Totah Gallery, 1988 St Paul's Gallery Leeds

EMMA SERGEANT
(painter, Agnew's) Won Imperial Tobacco/National Portrait Gallery competition. Solo exhibitions: 1987 Agnew's (portraits), 1988 Agnew's (paintings from Australia, Pakistan, Africa and England)

MELISSA SCOTT-MILLER
(painter, Albemarle Gallery) Born 1959, studied Slade, worked Spain, New York and Germany, lives and works London. Selected exhibitions: solo The Space Gallery, group Aquavella Gallery New York, *South Bank Picture Show* Royal Festival Hall, 1989 solo Albemarle Gallery

LOUISE SCULLION
(environmental sculptor) Born Helensburgh Scotland 1966, studied Glasgow, 1988 Cargill TravellingScholarship. Exhibitions/installations:1988 Third Eye Centre Glasgow, Glasgow Garden Festival

TERRY SHAVE
(painter) Born Suffolk 1952, studied Ipswich, Loughborough and Slade. Selected exhibitions: 1987 John Moores Liverpool, 1988 *Midland Contemporary Art* Warwick

YUKO SHIRAISHI
(painter, Edward Totah Gallery) Born Tokyo 1956, studied Chelsea, lives and works London. Selected exhibitions: 1984 solo Curwen Gallery, 1985-7 group Whitechapel Art Gallery, Space Gallery, Camden Arts Centre, Angela Flowers Gallery, 1988 solo Edward Totah Gallery

COLIN SMITH
(painter, Nicola Jacobs Gallery) Born Hertfordshire 1953, studied Falmouth and RCA, 1983-5 Harkness Fellowship New York. Solo exhibitions: 1986 Ruth Siegal New York, 1987 and 89 Nicola Jacobs

KATE SMITH
(installation artist, Matt's Gallery) Born 1954, studied London Poly and Goldsmiths. Installations: 1987 St George's Crypt and Matt's Gallery

KEIR SMITH
(environmental sculptor) Born 1950, lives London. Recent carvings of wood and stone sited at Stoke-on-Trent, Bath and Bristol

LANCE SMITH
(painter, Fabian Carlsson Gallery) Born 1950, studied Camberwell and RCA. Selected exhibitions: 1986 solo Fabian Carlsson and Arnolfini Bristol, 1987 Forum International Kunstmesse Zurich group Fabian Carlsson, 1988 touring England and Ireland 1989 solo Fabian Carlsson

ANDREW STAHL
(Paton Gallery) Born London 1954, studied Slade. Solo exhibitions: 1983 Air Gallery, 1984 and 88 Paton Gallery

SOPHIE DE STEMPEL
(painter, Albemarle Gallery) Born Kent 1960, studied City & Guilds. Solo exhibitions: 1986 Monolith Gallery, 1989 Albemarle Gallery

CHRISTOPHER STEVENS
(painter and set designer) Born Basingstoke 1956, studied Reading Univ, lives and works London. Selected exhibitions: 1986 solo Conduit Galleries, group Mall Galleries, 1988 solo Black Bull Gallery, *Abstraction* Los Angeles, group Riverside Studios

PHILIP STEVENS
(painter, Paton Gallery) Born Plymouth 1953, studied Plymouth, Wimbledon and RCA. Selected exhibitions: 1987 solo Paton Gallery, 1988 *Romantic Visions in British Painting* Camden Arts Centre

ANDRÉ STITT
(performance artist) Born Northern Ireland 1959, studied Belfast, lives London.

PAUL STOREY
(painter, Fischer Fine Art) Born London 1957, studied Birmingham Poly and RCA, lives and works Athens. Selected exhibitions: group Barbican Centre Art Gallery, 1987 RCA, Paton Gallery, Smiths Galleries 1987-8 *Germinations* (European touring)

MADELEINE STRINDBERG
(painter) Studied Byam Shaw, Goldsmiths and

L to R: Nigel Rolfe, *The Wings of Fear*, 1985, performance photograph; Louise Scullion, *Just Another Outdoor Game*, 1988, installation

RCA, 1988-9 artist-in-residence National Gallery. Selected exhibitions: 1987 Riverside Open, Athens International Barbican, *Spaces and Voids* Chisenhale Studios, Warwick Arts Trust

DAVID SUFF
(painter and printmaker, Piccadilly Gallery) Born 1955, studied Leeds University and RCA. Solo exhibitions: 1983 Piccadilly Gallery, Railings Gallery (prints)

VAJIRA SUGATHADASA
(painter) Born Sri Lanka 1955, England 1972, studied Slade, lives and works London. Solo exhibition: 1989 October Gallery

ANITA TAYLOR
(painter) Born Cheshire 1961, studied Mid-Cheshire College and RCA. Selected exhibitions: 1986 group Painters RCA Cheltenham, 1987 *Whitworth Young Contemporaries* Manchester, 1988 solo Trevelyan College Durham Univ, *An Artist's Residency* Durham Cathedral

FRASER TAYLOR
(painter, Thumb Gallery) Born Luton 1960, studied Glasgow and RCA. Selected exhibitions: 1985 solo L'Escargot, 1985-6 solos and group Thumb Gallery

STEPHEN TAYLOR WOODROW
(performance artist) Born 1960, studied Goldsmiths. Selected performances: 1986 *The Living Paintings*, 1988 *Going Bye-Byes*

ANNABELLE TEEDE
(painter) Born Zimbabwe 1956, studied Goldsmiths. Selected exhibitions: 1986 Camden Open, Riverside Open, 1988 Todd Gallery

BRIDGET TEMPEST
(printmaker) Born 1957, studied Ruskin Oxford, lives and works Oxford. Selected exhibitions: 1988 group Sue Rankin Gallery, Gallery El Taller Lima Peru, *Midlands Contemporary Art* Warwick

SIMON THOMAS
(environmental sculptor, Albemarle Gallery) Born 1960, studied fine art Plymouth and sculpture RCA, currently working in Cornwall. Selected exhibitions: *Sculptors of Fame and Promise* Chichester Cathedral *New Milestones* Dorchester County Museum, 1989 group Essex Univ, Ashton Court Parklands Bristol, Plymouth City Art Gallery, Crafts Council, solo Albemarle Gallery

MARION THOMSON
(painter) Born 1960, studied Univ of Newcastle, currently at RCA. Selected exhibitions: 1987 Flowerfield Gallery Portstewart, Chapel Gallery Swansea, 1988 Open Studios SAAC Cardiff, 1989 Gordon Gallery Londonderry

JAKE TILSON
(painter, Nigel Greenwood Gallery) Born 1958, studied Chelsea and RCA, lives and works in London. Selected exhibitions: 1986 Nigel Greenwood Gallery, 1988 Guggenheim Musum New York, *Exhibition Road* RCA

SUZANNE TREISTER
(painter, Edward Totah Gallery) Born England 1958, studied St Martin's and Chelsea. Selected exhibitions: 1985 solo Edward Totah Gallery, 1986-7 group Edward Totah Gallery, Riverside Studios, Camden Arts Centre, Edward Bates Gallery Chicago, 1988 solo Edward Totah Gallery

RODERICK TYE
(sculptor) Born 1957, studied Lanchester Poly, Ravensbourne, Leeds Poly, Slade and British School Rome. Selected exhibitions: 1986 *Five Festival Sculptures* Stoke-on-Trent City Art Gallery, 1986-7 group *The Golden Thread* Harris Museum and Art Gallery Preston and touring.

KATHERINE VIRGILIS
(painter, Thumb Gallery) Born Houston Texas 1954, studied Ravensbourne and RCA. Selected exhibitions: 1985 *Ceramics and Wall Tapestries* Fitzwilliam Cambridge, 1986 *Working with Paper* RIBA, 1988 solo Thumb Gallery

CARLOS VILLENEUVA
(architect, painter and installation artist, Albemarle Gallery) Born Caracas Venezuela 1957, studied Architectural Association, lives and works London. Selected exhibitions: 1985 Venice Biennale, Air Gallery, 1986 Fruitmarket Gallery Edinburgh, 1987 Richard Pomeroy Gallery, Institute of Contemporary Art Boston, 1989 Albemarle Gallery

NICHOLAS VOLLEY
(painter, Browse & Darby) Born Grimsby 1950, studied Grimsby and Slade. Selected exhibitions: 1986 and 89 Browse & Darby

RICHARD WALKER
(painter, Thumb Gallery) Born Yorkshire 1954, studied Camberwell and Chelsea. Solo exhibitions: 1988 Minsky's Gallery, Thumb Gallery, Madison Galleries Los Angeles

JONATHAN WALLER
(painter, Paton Gallery) Born Stratford-upon-Avon 1956, studied Lanchester Poly and Chelsea. Selected exhibitions: 1986 & 1988 solo Paton Gallery, 1989 group *New British Painting* Cincinnati

MARK WALLINGER
(mixed-media/installation artist, Anthony Reynolds Gallery) Born 1959 Essex, studied Loughton, Chelsea and Goldsmiths. Solo exhibitions: 1988 Nottingham Castle Museum, Riverside Studios, Anthony Reynolds Gallery

FRANK WATKINS
(mixed-media painter) Born Glanamman Carmarthenshire 1951, studied Carmarthen, Newport, Cardiff, lives and works Ammanford Dyfed. Solo exhibitions: 1984 *Homage* Oriel Cardiff, 1988 Artsite Bath

ALAN WATSON
(painter) Born St Andrews Scotland 1957, studied Duncan of Jordanstone Dundee.

ALISON WATT
(painter, The Scottish Gallery) Born 1965, studied Glasgow, lives and works Scotland. 1987 National Portrait Gallery/John Player Portrait Award

ELAINE WATT
(painter) Born 1965, studied Mabel Fletcher Tech Liverpool and Birmingham Poly. Selected exhibitions: 1987 group Perry Bar Gallery, 1988 Porl-Porl Gallery Leeds

RICHARD ANTHONY WEBB
(painter) Born 1963, studied Camberwell and RCA. Selected exhibitions: 1988 Graduates Oxford Gallery, 1989 two-person Cadogan Contemporary

PETER WHITE
(painter) Born 1959, studied Edinburgh. Selected exhibitions: 1988 Manchester City Open, Society of Aberdeen Artists Acorn Gallery Birmingham, Square Gallery

KATE WHITEFORD
(painter/installations) Born Glasgow 1952, studied Glasgow Univ, lives and works London. Selected solo exhibitions: 1986 solo Riverside Studios, 1987 solo Fruitmarket Gallery Edinburgh, solo Graeme Murray Gallery Edinburgh, group *Vigorous Imagination* Scottish National Gallery of Modern Art, sculpture for Calton Hill Edinburgh, 1988-9 solo Whitechapel Art Gallery

ALUN WILLIAMS
(painter) Born Manchester 1961, studied Univ of Wales, Ecole Nationale des Beaux-Arts de Bourges France, Blackheath and Goldsmiths, 1983-4 John Skeaping RA Memorial Artist's Residency Castries France. Selected exhibitions: 1986 OYB Gallery, Le Faste Fou Paris, 1987 Goldsmiths Gallery, *Icons* Mario Flecha Gallery, 1989 l'Ecole de Nimes France

ANDREW WILLIAMS
(painter, 369 Gallery Edinburgh) Born Barry S Wales 1954, studied Edinburgh, lives and works Edinburgh and the Dordogne. Solo exhibitions: 1986 and 89 369 Gallery Edinburgh

AUBREY WILLIAMS
Selected exhibition: 198 Gallery

EMRYS WILLIAMS
(painter, Benjamin Rhodes Gallery) Born Liverpool 1958, studied Slade, lives and works Colwyn Bay Wales, member of *56 Group Wales*. Selected exhibitions: solos 1986 and 89 Benjamin Rhodes Gallery, 1987 group Serpentine Summer Show II, *The Other Landscape* Southampton City Art Gallery, 1989 *Ways of Telling* Mostyn Art Gallery Llandudno

GERRARD WILLIAMS
(installation artist, Anthony d'Offay) Born Manchester 1959, lives and works London. Selected exhibitions: 1987 solo Interim Art, Whitechapel Art Gallery, 1989 group Anthony d'Offay

JANET WILLIAMS

(painter) Studied North Staffordshire Poly and Slade. Selected exhibitions: 1988 *Midlands Contemporary Art* Warwick

LOIS WILLIAMS
(sculptor) Born Denbigh 1953, studied Wrexham, Manchester and Goldsmiths, member of Artemisia group of women artists. Selected exhibitions: 1987 solo St Paul's Gallery Leeds, group *Conceptual Clothing* Ikon Gallery Birmingham 1988 *The Wedding* Mappin Gallery Sheffield

MOIRA WILLS
(silkscreen printmaker and illustrator) Born Surrey 1961, studied West Surrey and Camberwell. Group exhibitions: 1987 and 88 Prism Gallery Brighton, 1988 Café Casbar, Smith's Gallery, *New Decorative Art* Harrods London

ANTHONY WILSON
(video/performance artist/photographer, Matt's Gallery) Born 1959 Blackpool, studied Brighton Poly and Goldsmiths, lives and works London. Solo exhibitions: 1987 *Satellite* Riverside Studios, 1989 Anthony Reynolds Gallery

RICHARD WILSON
(sculptor/performance artist, Matt's Gallery) Born 1953 London, studied London College of Printing, Hornsey and Reading Univ, member of Bow Gamelan Ensemble with Anne Bean and Paul Burwell. Solo exhibitions: 1986 Stoke Garden Festival, Venice Biennale *Aperto*, Ikon Gallery Birmingham, 1987 Matt's Gallery, installation inside Tyne Bridge Newcastle, 1989 Brandts Kunsthallen Odense Denmark, Arnolfini Bristol, Matt's Gallery, Museum of Modern Art Oxford

ADRIAN WISZNIEWSKI
(artist, Nigel Greenwood Gallery) Born Glasgow 1958, studied Mackintosh School of Architecture Glasgow and Glasgow, 1988 artist-in-residence Walker Art Gallery Liverpool. Selected exhibitions: 1986 group Washington Gallery Glasgow, Nigel Greenwood, 1987 solo Walker Art Gallery Liverpool, group *Vigorous Imagination* Scottish National Gallery of Modern Art

CHRISTOPHER WOOD
(painter, Sue Williams) Born 1961, studied Leeds Poly and Chelsea. Selected exhibitions: 1987 Angela Flowers Gallery, 1988 Manchester Academy of Fine Art, 1989 solo Sue Williams

VINCENT WOROPAY
(sculptor, Fabian Carlsson Gallery) Born London 1951, studied Portsmouth, Brighton Poly, Slade and British School Rome. Selected exhibitions: 1987 solo Artsite Gallery Bath, group Fabian Carlsson Gallery, 1988 solo Bluecoat Gallery Liverpool, Fabian Carlsson, group Powis Castle

ANTHONY ZYCH
(painter in varnish and mineral pigments, Albemarle Gallery) Born 1958, studied Kingston and Camberwell, philosophy St Andrew's Univ, fine art Slade. Solo exhibitions: 1986 Bernard Jacobson Gallery, 1989 Albemarle Gallery

L to R: Watkins, *Fragment of Painting*, 1984, mixed media; A Wilson, *Satellite*, 1986, performance; P Williams, *Symptoms of Being*, 1988, mixed media